Peruvian Cookbook

*Traditional Peruvian Recipes
Made Easy*

www.grizzlypublishing.com

Table of Contents

INTRODUCTION 1

CHAPTER ONE: PERUVIAN BREAKFAST RECIPES 3

TACU TACU (BEANS AND RICE) 3
PAPAS A LA HUANCAINA (POTATOES IN A SPICY CHEESE SAUCE) 5
CHICHARRONES SANDWICH WITH SALSA CRIOLLA 7
CEVICHE PERUANO 9
PERUVIAN CAUSA (SPICY POTATO-LAYERED WITH MEAT) 11
DESAYUNO LURÍN 13
LOCRO ECUATORIANO (POTATO-CHEESE SOUP) 15
PERUVIAN QUINOA PORRIDGE 16
FRIJOLES ESCABECHADOS 17
GACHAS DE ESTILO PERUANO (PERUVIAN STYLE PORRIDGE)........................ 19
HUEVOS TRIPADOS PERUVIAN TOMATOES AND EGG NOODLES 22
HUEVOS A LA RABONA 25
CACHANGAS 26
TROPICAL FRUIT SALAD WITH BEE POLLEN 28
PERUVIAN TAMALES CRIOLLOS 29

CHAPTER TWO: PERUVIAN LUNCH RECIPES 32

PERUVIAN PALTA RELLENA 32
PARIHUELA (PERUVIAN SEAFOOD SOUP) 33
GRILLED PERUVIAN CHICKEN WRAPS 36
PERUVIAN AVOCADO TOSTADA 38
QUINUA CON COLINABO Y CEBOLLA PERLA (QUINOA WITH KOHLRABI AND PEARL ONIONS) . 40
SEITAN SALTADO (PERUVIAN POTATO STIR-FRY) 42
PAN CON CHICHARRON (PERUVIAN PORK ROLL) 44
SALCHIPAPAS (PERUVIAN SAUSAGES AND POTATOES)................................ 46
PERUVIAN CRISP POTATOES STUFFED WITH SPICED BEEF AND PECANS 47
ENSALADA MIRAFLORES 49
CEBICHE DE ATUN (PERUVIAN CANNED TUNA CEVICHE) 51
SALTADO DE VAINITAS 52
PAPA RELLENA (PERUVIAN STUFFED POTATOES) 54
PERUVIAN CEVICHE.. 56
CAU CAU (PERUVIAN TRIPE STEW) 58
ARROZ TAPADO (PERUVIAN MEAT-FILLED RICE) 61

CHAPTER THREE: PERUVIAN DINNER RECIPES 63

AJI DE GALLINA (PERUVIAN SPICY CREAMED CHICKEN) 63

SANCOCHADO (PERUVIAN BRAISED BEEF AND VEGETABLES WITH SALSA SAUTÉ) 65

ARROZ CON POLLO (CHICKEN AND RICE)...68

POLLO SALTADO (PERUVIAN-STYLE CHICKEN STIR-FRY) 70

ARROZ CHAUFA (PERUVIAN FRIED RICE) 72

SOPA CRIOLLA (PERUVIAN BEEF NOODLE SOUP).....................................74

SUDADO DE PESCADO CRIOLLO (PERUVIAN STEAMED FISH) 76

SALMON TARTARE PERUVIAN STYLE 78

SECO DE CORDERO (PERUVIAN LAMB STEW)...80

PERUVIAN SEAFOOD SOUP 82

THE HIRSHON PERUVIAN CEVICHE..84

GRILLED PERUVIAN CHICKEN..86

PACHAMANCA A LA OLLA 88

TALLARINES VERDES (PERUVIAN-STYLE PESTO)....................................91

PERUVIAN SOPA SECA 93

CARAPULCRA (FREEZE DRIED POTATOES WITH PORK) 95

ESCABECHE DE PESCADO (PERUVIAN PICKLED FISH)...............................97

PERUVIAN CHICKEN STEW 100

POLLO A LA BRASA (PERUVIAN GRILLED CHICKEN) 102

PERUVIAN CILANTRO RICE 105

OCOPA CON CAMARONES (SHRIMP IN OCOPA SAUCE) 106

ANTICUCHOS (PERUVIAN CHICKEN KEBABS) 108

SECO DE CERDO (PORK IN CILANTRO SAUCE) 110

CHAPTER FOUR: PERUVIAN DESSERT RECIPES 112

TURRON DOÑA PEPA (ANISE COOKIE BAR WITH CANDY SYRUP) 112

MAZAMORRA MORADA (PURPLE CORN PUDDING) 114

ARROZ ZAMBITO (DARK RICE PUDDING) 116

PERUVIAN ALFAJORES WITH MANJAR BLANCO 118

PICARONES (SWEET POTATO DOUGHNUT)...120

SUSPIRO LIMENO (PERUVIAN CUSTARD) 122

FRUIT ESPUMA (GELATIN FOAM)..124

TRES LECHES (PERUVIAN THREE MILKS) 125

PIE DE LIMON (PERUVIAN LIME PIE)...127

CREMA VOLTEADA (PERUVIAN CRÈME CARAMEL) 129

ARROZ CON LECHE (PERUVIAN RICE PUDDING)...................................131

SUSPIRO A LA LIMENA (PERUVIAN CARAMEL PUDDING) 132

PERUVIAN CARAMEL SANDWICH COOKIES 134

HUMITAS DE MOTE (DRIED CORN HUMITAS)......................................136

CONCLUSION..137

Introduction

First and foremost, I want to give a huge thank you for purchasing my book, 'Peruvian Cookbook: Traditional Peruvian Recipes Made Easy.'

Many don't realize it, but Peru is truly one of the most culturally rich countries on this amazing planet. With a unique history and a vast depth of migration and culture, this amazing country has developed into a hub for travelers and holiday goers alike.

But it's important to note that this great place has so much more to offer than amazing scenery and gorgeous landscapes – it offers hiking, super friendly people, and a relaxed way of life rarely seen in the western world.

And of course, I should also add that the food is absolutely incredible!

Like a number of other countries, Peru has been heavily influenced by the immigrants that once populated it. While this has obviously had an impact on its hospitable culture, it has had an even larger impact on their cuisine.

Heavily influenced by a unique combination of the indigenous Inca, the Spanish, the Chinese, and the Japanese, there is a reason that traditional Peruvian cooking stands alone as some of the most interesting on the planet.

Modern day Peruvian cooking now revolves around the implementation of three traditional staples, corn, potatoes, and Chile peppers. While as standalone ingredients these three may sound a little underwhelming, when combined into the numerous dishes' native to Peru, they become so much more than a simple ingredient – they become an absolute delight to the taste buds.

Moreover, with the heavy Spanish influence placed upon this great nation, Peru has slowly integrated pork, fish, and poultry into its cooking regime, in conjunction with numerous traditional Spanish cooking methodologies.

And the result?

A grouping of rich and interesting flavors and textures that can only be found in this amazing country.

Over time, the local food and its preparation has evolved to become one the most important parts of Peruvian culture. It is thought of as so much more than just simply 'cooking', but rather as a personal way to express the Peruvian history and the collective identity of its population.

With this all this in mind, Peruvian cuisine is among the most varied (and dare I say, best) in the world.

It not only reflects that history and background of this great country, but also provides a representation of its three main geographical zones; the coast, the Andean highlands and the jungle. This amazing collaboration between history, culture, and location and has created a cuisine unlike any other – and this amazing mix of flavors, textures, and smells, will leave its mark for years to come.

So, although Peruvian cuisine has only truly been recognized on an international scale over the last few years, it has quickly made an imprint on all who taste it.

In short, prepare to be amazed!

Chapter One: Peruvian Breakfast Recipes

Tacu Tacu (Beans and Rice)

Serves: 4

Ingredients:

- 1 x 400 g tin of haricot beans
- 300 g long-grain white rice
- 4 medium-large free-range eggs
- 2 cloves of garlic
- 1 plantain
- 1 onion
- 1 fresh red chili
- olive oil
- hot chili sauce

Method:

1. Start by cooking the rice according to packet instructions, then drain and cool.
2. Peel and slice the plantain about 1.5cm thick. Peel and finely chop the garlic and onion, then finely slice the chili. Drain the beans.
3. Add a couple of good lugs of oil to a large non-stick frying pan over a medium heat and fry the plantain for a few minutes on each side, or until golden and crisp. Set aside and keep warm.
4. Return the pan, with any leftover oil, to the heat. Fry the garlic, onion and chili over a medium-low heat for 5 to 10 minutes, or until softened and lightly golden.

5. Stir in 1 tablespoon of hot chili sauce, the beans and cooled rice.
6. Turn the heat up to high and fry the mixture until the rice is piping hot and beginning to crisp up, stirring regularly. Stop stirring for the last couple of minutes to let it get golden and crisp on the bottom – this is your tacu tacu! Transfer to a plate and set aside.
7. Add a little more oil to the same pan and place over a medium heat. Fry the eggs, adding the plantain for the last minute to warm through.
8. Divide the tacu tacu among your plates, making sure everyone gets some of that lovely crispy bottom, and top each portion with a fried egg, some crispy plantain and an extra dash of chili sauce, if you like.

Papas a la Huancaina (Potatoes in a Spicy Cheese Sauce)

Serves: 8

Ingredients:

- 14 ounces queso blanco (fresh white cheese)
- 8 yukon gold potatoes
- 6 medium-large black olives (halved)
- 4 leaves lettuce (or more to taste)
- 4 yellow chili peppers
- 2 garlic cloves
- 2 medium-large hard-boiled eggs (halved)
- 1 teaspoon olive oil
- ½ cup vegetable oil
- 2 tablespoons heavy whipping cream, or more as needed (optional)

Method:

1. First, bring a large pot of water to a boil. Add the potatoes; cook until tender when pierced with a fork, about 30-45 minutes. Drain and let cool, about 15 minutes.
2. Heat olive oil in a small saucepan. Add yellow chili peppers and garlic cloves; cook and stir until lightly golden, about 2 minutes.
3. Transfer chili peppers and garlic cloves to a blender. Add queso blanco and vegetable oil; blend until smooth. Thin with heavy cream until a creamy consistency is reached.
4. Arrange lettuce leaves on a large platter. Cut potatoes in half and place on top. Pour sauce over potatoes.
5. Garnish with hard-boiled eggs and black olives.

Note:

- Habanero or serrano chile peppers can be substituted for the yellow chile peppers.
- Substitute feta cheese for the queso blanco if desired.
- Substitute milk for the heavy whipping cream if desired.

Chicharrones Sandwich with Salsa Criolla

Serves: 2-4

Ingredients:

Chicharrones de chancho (crispy pork cubes):

- 1 lb. pork spare ribs (cut into 2-inch sections)
- 1 teaspoon salt
- 1 tablespoon lime juice
- 1 teaspoon oil
- ½ teaspoon ground cumin

Salsa criolla:

- 3-4 tablespoons lime juice
- 2 cups red onion (coarsely chopped)
- 1 teaspoon chopped/paste aji amarillo, remove seeds if chopping.
- 1 teaspoon salt
- 1 tablespoon cilantro (chopped)

Method:

For the Chicharrones de chancho (crispy pork cubes):

1. First, mix all ingredients except oil in a bowl and let marinate for 15 minutes.
2. Heat oil in a skillet or a pan on low heat.
3. Add the pork and fry at low temperatures for about 30 minutes.
4. The pork is done when the meat is brown and crisp with all of the fat cooked off.

5. Drain pieces over paper towels and serve as soon as possible.

For the salsa criolla:

1. Combine all ingredients by hand, or
2. Pulse all ingredients in a food processor to make a coarse salsa.
3. Serve immediately.

Ceviche Peruano

Serves: 8

Ingredients:

- 1-pound fresh tilapia (cut into 1/2-inch pieces)
- 1-pound medium shrimp (peeled, deveined, and cut into 1/2-inch pieces)
- 2 medium-large potatoes
- 2 medium sweet potatoes
- 1 red onion (cut into thin strips)
- 1 cup fresh lime juice
- 1 pinch ground cumin
- 1 clove garlic (minced)
- 1 habanero pepper (seeded and minced)
- 1 bibb or Boston lettuce (separated into leaves)
- ½ stalk celery (sliced)
- ¼ cup lightly packed cilantro leaves
- salt and pepper to taste

Method:

1. Start with placing the potatoes and sweet potatoes in a saucepan and cover with water. Simmer until the potatoes are easily pierced with a fork, then drain, and set aside to cool to room temperature.
2. Place the sliced onion in a bowl of warm water, let stand 10 minutes, then drain and set aside.
3. In the meantime, place the lime juice, celery, cilantro, and cumin into the bowl of a blender, and puree until smooth. Pour this mixture into a large glass bowl, and stir in the garlic and habanero pepper.

4. Season with salt and pepper, then stir in the diced tilapia and shrimp.
5. Set aside to marinate for an hour, stirring occasionally. The seafood is done once it turns firm and opaque.
6. To serve, peel the potatoes and cut into slices. Stir the onions into the fish mixture. Line serving bowls with lettuce leaves. Spoon the ceviche with its juice into the bowls and garnish with slices of potato.

Peruvian Causa (Spicy Potato-Layered with Meat)

Serves: 8

Ingredients:

- 8 medium russet potatoes (peeled)
- 3 hard-boiled eggs (thinly sliced)
- 2 (5 ounce) cans tuna (drained)
- 2 medium avocados (cut into thin strips)
- 2 tablespoons aji amarillo (minced)
- 1 small red onion (diced small)
- ½ cup vegetable oil (or as needed)
- ½ cup mayonnaise (divided)
- salt and pepper to taste

Method:

1. First, place the potatoes into a large pot and cover with salted water; bring to a boil. Reduce heat to medium-low and simmer until tender, about 20 minutes. Drain.
2. Mash potatoes with a ricer or hand mixer until smooth. Gradually stir in oil until potatoes come together; add aji amarillo, salt, and pepper.
3. Cool potato mixture in the refrigerator, about 20 minutes.
4. Stir tuna, onion, and ¼ cup mayonnaise together in a bowl.
5. Line a casserole dish with plastic wrap. Spread ½ the potato mixture on the bottom of the dish. Spread 2 tablespoons mayonnaise over the potatoes, spread the tuna mixture over the mayonnaise, and place the avocado slices in a single layer on top of the tuna mixture.

6. Spread the remaining ½ of potato mixture over the avocados, and top with remaining 2 tablespoons mayonnaise. Place sliced eggs over the top. Cover casserole dish with plastic wrap and refrigerate until firm, about 30 minutes.
7. Invert casserole dish onto a serving dish or baking sheet to remove potato casserole from dish.
8. Remove plastic wrap and cut casserole into squares.

Desayuno Lurín

Serves: 4

Ingredients:

For the pork belly:

- 4 lb. pork meat (preferably ribs)
- ½ lb. onion (julienned)
- salt to taste

For the tamales:

- 1 lb. chicken (shredded)
- 10 onion (chopped)
- 10 corn cobs (grated)
- ½ lb. lard
- 1/8 lb. toasted peanuts
- 12 black olives (pits removed)
- 4 mirasol peppers (deveined and seeds removed)
- 3 medium eggs (boiled)
- 3 garlic cloves
- plantain leaves (washed)
- salsa criolla, to taste
- salt and pepper, to taste

Method:

For the pork belly:

1. In a pot of water, boil the pork meat until all the water evaporates and the meat begins to brown with its own fat. Once the meat has fried in its own fat and it looks browned, drain the excess fat.

1. Serve immediately with a side of fried sweet potato.

For the tamales:

1. Cook the grated corn in a pot of water for 5 minutes. Drain the water. Process the corn with a little vegetable oil until it makes a paste.
2. In a frying pan add 2 tablespoons of lard, add corn paste and stir continuously. Add chicken and remaining ingredients, including chicken stock. Cook until the corn paste is fully cooked and has thickened.
3. Add a little of the cooked corn mixture to a plantain leaf, a piece of chicken, ¼ of boiled egg, toasted corn and 3 olives. Cover it with some more of the corn mixture. Fold the tamale and cover it with strips of plantain leaves.
4. Once you have the tamales ready, cook them in a large pot of water for 1 hour. Once ready serve them with salsa criolla.
5. Invert casserole dish onto a serving dish or baking sheet to remove potato casserole from dish.

Note:

- Serve the breakfast platter with a side of French bread and café con leche to enjoy the full Lurín Breakfast experience at home.

Locro Ecuatoriano (Potato-Cheese Soup)

Serves: 4

Ingredients:

- 1 ½ pounds potatoes (or more to taste, peeled and diced)
- 4 cups chicken stock
- 3 cloves garlic (or more to taste, minced)
- 1 cup milk
- 1 cup shredded Muenster cheese
- ½ onion (minced)
- ¼ cup butter
- salt and pepper to taste

Method:

1. Start by melting the butter in a large pot over medium heat. Cook and stir onion and garlic in hot butter until onion is translucent, 5 to 7 minutes.
2. Stir potatoes, chicken stock, and milk with the onion mixture; season with salt and pepper. Bring the liquid to a boil, reduce heat to low, and cook at a simmer until potatoes are tender and falling apart, 30 to 45 minutes.
3. Mash potatoes lightly to help thicken the soup, while keeping some chunks in the soup.
4. Remove pot from heat and stir cheese into the soup to melt.

Note:
- Water can be used in place of chicken stock, if needed.
- Either queso fresco or mozzarella cheese can replace the Muenster cheese in this recipe.

Peruvian Quinoa Porridge

Serves: 4

Ingredients:

- 2 tablespoons coconut sugar (or honey)
- 2 cups rice milk (or Brazil nut milk)
- 1 cup quinoa
- 1 cup amaranth
- 1 teaspoon cloves
- 1 teaspoon cinnamon
- 1 scoop vanilla protein
- 1 teaspoon sea salt

Method:

1. First, heat the nut milk with cloves and cinnamon. Slowly add coconut sugar to it.
2. After boiling for about 15 minutes, strain out the ingredients, and allow the nut milk to cool.
3. Cook the quinoa and amaranth separately in a pan.
4. Once the grains are done, transfer as much as needed to the milk to reach desired consistency.
5. Using a ladle, you can stir the mixture.
6. Add the vanilla protein at this point.
7. You can serve this warm or store it in the refrigerator and serve it cold.

Note:
- You can change the consistency of the porridge by adding more grains or even chia seeds to it.
- Or serve it as a light porridge by adding more nut milk to it.

Frijoles Escabechados

Serves: 5

Ingredients:

- 4 slices bacon
- 2 cups dried black beans (such as turtle beans, or 3 cups canned)
- 1 chile pepper (aji Amarillo, or other fresh chile pepper, seeds removed, sliced thinly)
- 1 tablespoon minced garlic
- 1 tablespoon chili pepper (aji panca, paste)
- 1 teaspoon cumin
- 1 packet sazon goya (with cilantro and tomato)
- 1 large white onion
- ¼ rice wine vinegar
- salt and pepper to taste

Method:

1. First, soak dried beans overnight.
2. Drain and cover with clean water, and bring to a simmer. Add a slice of bacon, and simmer beans until tender. Drain, reserving about 1 cup of the cooking liquid.
3. Add remaining 3 pieces of bacon to a large skillet and fry until crispy. Remove from pan, crumble, and set aside.
4. Slice onions into thin half-moon shaped pieces ("a la pluma"). Add onion and garlic to the same skillet with the aji chile pepper paste, cumin, and the sazon Goya, and cook them in the bacon grease over medium heat until they are golden brown, soft, and translucent. Add the sliced chile pepper and sauté for several minutes more.

5. Puree half of the beans in a blender with the reserved cooking liquid. Add the pureed beans to the skillet and simmer, stirring, for several minutes.
6. Add the remaining beans, the vinegar, and the crumbled bacon. Cook, stirring until beans are heated through.
7. Serve warm with white rice.

Gachas De Estilo Peruano (Peruvian Style Porridge)

Serves: 6

Ingredients:

Manjar blanco & panthers milk:

- 200 ml single cream
- 200 ml condensed milk
- 5 cm green chili (frozen & finely grated)
- 5 cm red chili (frozen & finely grated)
- 5 cm cinnamon stick
- 4 cloves
- 3 tablespoons pisco
- 3 tablespoons lime juice
- 1 teaspoon vanilla bean paste
- pinch sea salt
- a squeeze of mango juice

Spiced coconut porridge:

- 1500 ml rude health coconut drink
- 300 g rude health 5 grain 5 seed porridge
- 6 tablespoons coconut sugar
- 6 tablespoons desiccated coconut
- 3 tablespoons vanilla bean paste
- 1 tablespoon ground cinnamon
- pinch salt

Candied cashews, mango & sweet potato ceviche & mango crisps:

- 150 g granulated sugar (plus extra for dusting)
- 100 g cashew nuts

- 100 ml water
- 1 lime (zested)
- ¾ mango (brunoise)
- ¾ cooked sweet potato (brunoise)
- ¼ mango (thinly sliced)

Method:

1. Combine ingredients for manjar blanco in a small pan the day before serving. Bring to the boil and reduce the heat to low. Simmer, stirring often for 2-3 hours until thick and caramelized. Taste and adjust the spicing to your liking then leave to cool and refrigerate.
2. For the lime, place 100 g of sugar in a pan with water and bring to the boil.
3. Whilst this is heating, pour a kettle of water over the lime zest and soak for 30 seconds. Drain, refresh in cold water and repeat (this will remove any bitterness).
4. Boil the zest in the sugar syrup for 5 minutes, drain, sprinkle with sugar and leave to set on a rack. Once set, store in an airtight jar.
5. For the cashews, place the sugar in a wide pan over a medium heat to dissolve the sugar. Swirl the pan but do not stir. Once the sugar is bubbling, leave to turn amber in color and add the cashews. Swirl to coat and pour onto baking parchment. Leave to set and break up when cool. Store in an airtight jar.
6. Mix all the porridge ingredients in a large pan and soak for 10 minutes.
7. Place pan on a medium heat and allow to cook for 15-20 minutes until the oats are tender but maintain a bit of bite (top the oats up with water if they become too thick).

8. Meanwhile, mix the ingredients for the panthers milk in a bowl and use to marinade the ceviche ingredients for 10 minutes.

9. Once the porridge is ready, serve, topped with ceviche (draining off some of the panthers milk before serving), Manjar Blanco, candied cashews and lime zest, and mango crisps.

Huevos Tripados Peruvian Tomatoes and Egg Noodles

Serves: 6

Ingredients:

Noodles:

- 9 medium-large eggs
- 1 tablespoon clarified butter *(see note)*
- ½ teaspoon coarse sea salt
- ¼ teaspoon ground black pepper
- ½ cup grated Mexican Manchego cheese
- 1/8 cup water biscuits (finely crushed)

Tomato sauce:

- 9 plum tomatoes
- 3 tablespoons olive oil
- 2 teaspoons ground fennel seeds
- 2 large cloves garlic (minced)
- 1 medium onion (minced)
- 1 teaspoon paprika
- 1 teaspoon cayenne pepper
- 1 bay leaf
- 1 tablespoon coarse sea salt
- 1 small carrot (grated)
- ½ small bunch fresh basil (leaves only, coarsely chopped)

Method:

1. Start by breaking the eggs one by one, into a small bowl, then slide them into a large mixing bowl. Add ½ cup cold

water, the salt, and pepper. Whisk together until evenly blended, then stir in the grated cheese and the crushed biscuits.

2. Brush a 10-inch nonstick skillet with a little clarified butter and place it over medium heat. Pour ½ cup of the well stirred egg mixture into the pan and immediately swirl it to coat the base of the pan evenly.

3. Cook until the mixture has set, about 1 ½ minutes. Using a long, wide, spatula, turn the omelet to the other side to cook for a few seconds more. Slide the omelet out onto a plate and continue making omelets in the same way until you have used all the mixture. You should have about 4 omelets stacked on top of each other. Cover and keep warm.

4. Blanch, peel, core and seed all the tomatoes, placing all the seeds in a strainer set over a bowl. Coarsely chop 6 of the tomatoes and set them aside. Cut the remaining 3 tomatoes in half lengthwise and puree them in a blender or a food processor.

5. Press the seeds in the strainer to extract as much juice as possible. Discard the seeds and set the juice aside separately. In a large heavy casserole that can be brought to the table, heat the olive oil over low heat and add the onion. Cook, stirring, for about 7 minutes, or until translucent, then stir in the garlic, paprika, cayenne pepper, bay leaf, fennel, and salt and cook for 2 minutes more, or until the garlic releases its aroma.

6. Add the grated carrot and the juice from the tomato seeds, increase the heat to medium high and cook until all of the liquid has evaporated, about 8 minutes. Add the chopped tomatoes and cook for 10 minutes, stirring occasionally, until the sauce is chunky and thick, then

add the pureed tomatoes and cook just until heated through. Remove from the heat.

7. Stack 2 of the omelets, roll them up tightly, and cut crosswise into 1/4-inch-wide noodles, keeping them rolled up. Repeat with the other 2 omelets. Arrange the rolls of noodles in overlapping circles on top of the tomato sauce and scatter the chopped basil over the top.

8. To serve, toss the noodles gently with the tomato sauce and transfer to individual plates.

Note:

- **To clarify butter:** Melt 1 cup butter in a heavy saucepan over medium heat. Simmer until the butter foams, then skim and discard the white froth that forms at the top. Carefully pour the remaining butter through a double thickness of damp cheesecloth, leaving the white sediment at the bottom of the pan. (Yield: ¾ cup)

Huevos a la Rabona

Serves: 2

Ingredients:

- 4 medium eggs
- 4 bread slices
- 2 tablespoons rocoto (or any red hot chili pepper, finely diced)
- 2 tablespoons vegetable oil
- 1 tablespoon vinegar or lime juice
- 1 tablespoon oil
- ½ red onion (finely diced)
- salt and pepper to taste
- 2 tablespoons cilantro leaves, chopped (optional)

Method:

1. First, put the onion and rocoto in a bowl, cover with cold water and rest for 10 minutes. Drain well.
2. Transfer onion and rocoto mix to a bowl and add cilantro leaves, salt, pepper, vinegar and 1 tablespoon oil. Reserve.
3. Toast the bread in the oven or a skillet until lightly golden. Put 2 slices in each plate. (You can also fry it with some oil, which is the original way of making this dish).
4. Heat the vegetable oil in a small frying pan and fry the eggs, sunny-side-up. Season with salt.
5. Put a fried egg on top of each toast.
6. Put a tablespoon of the onion mixture on top of each fried egg, and serve immediately.

Cachangas

Serves: 2

Ingredients:

- 1 ½ cups flour
- 2 tablespoons salt (plus more for sprinkling, optional)
- 1 tablespoons oil + more for frying
- ¾ cup water
- ½ tablespoon baking powder

Method:

1. Start by mixing all the dry ingredients in a medium bowl (flour, salt, baking powder if using).
2. Make a small well in the middle and add oil, mix a little with a fork.
3. Add water slowly – maybe add half of it and mix well. Then add a little bit more, until you reach the right consistency. You want the dough to be dry enough to handle, but wet enough that there is some elasticity in it. It's easier if you work the dough with your hands.
4. Form small balls (about the size of a golf ball) and set them aside. You should have about 8 – 10 balls. If less that's alright, your cachangas will be slightly bigger; if more, then your cachangas will be slightly smaller.
5. Pour some oil – enough to cover the base – on a frying pan. (The key here is to NOT BURN the oil). I can cook the cachangas on med-high (#8 on the knob/dial thing) without burning the oil, but still getting them thoroughly cooked and golden brown.

6. When the oil is nice and warm, start flattening the dough balls. You can squish them between your palms and then carefully expand them from the contours. If the dough rips a little, that's ok. It adds character and makes that section extra crunchy. They need to be somewhat thin so they can cook fast and not burn.
7. Sprinkle some salt on cachangas as they are cooking (optional)
8. Cook each side until they are golden brown. (I use a fork to turn them over – sometimes spatulas just don't work)
9. Enjoy your cachangas plain, with a little bit of salt sprinkled on top, or with honey or maple syrup poured on.

Tropical Fruit Salad with Bee Pollen

Serves: 2

Ingredients:

- 1 ripe mango (cubed)
- 1 cup papaya (cubed)
- 1 cup pineapple (cubed)
- 1 banana (sliced)
- 2 tablespoons coconut flakes
- 1 teaspoon bee pollen
- ½ orange (juiced)

Method:

1. Gently combine all of the fruit in a medium bowl.
2. Pour the orange juice over the fruit and stir gently.
3. Sprinkle with coconut flakes and bee pollen.

Peruvian Tamales Criollos

Serves: 35

Ingredients:

- 2 ½ pounds pork chops (no bones)
- 2 pounds white corn (peeled)
- 1-pound banana leaves (cut in 12-inch X 18-inch pieces)
- ½ pound fresh pork fat
- 100 grams roasted peanuts (ground)
- 100 grams black olives (preferably Peruvian)
- 50 grams sesame seeds (roasted)
- 10 ears cob corn on the (without kernels)
- 8 garlic cloves (fresh, peeled)
- 6 medium egg yolks
- 6 red chili (dried)
- 2 chilies (fresh yellow, roasted, Aji MIrasol)
- 2 hard-boiled egg (cut into eight pieces, wedges, not slices)
- 2 tablespoons vinegar
- 2 cups water
- ½ teaspoon ground pepper
- ½ teaspoon ground cumin

Method:

1. The original recipe is done with Peruvian white corn, it has the biggest grain in the world and it can be cut off the cob and peeled to prepare for the recipe, but you can substitute it for just the frozen bags that you can find in any grocery store. Preferably, grind the corn using a grinding machine, not blender (as last resource you can

blend the corn in a good blender using very little liquid). Set aside.

2. Blend the salt, pepper, cumin, vinegar and red dried chili (previously roasted and deveined).
3. Cut the meat into medium sized pieces and marinade for about an hour in the previous mix.
4. Brown the meat in a teaspoon of lard, add the left-over marinade and the two cups of water, and bring it to a boil, simmer to cook for two hours. Remove the pieces of meat and set aside.
5. Add the broth to the corn, the rest of the lard, peanuts, sesame seeds, 6 yolks and the glass of Pisco (if you can't find Peruvian Pisco leave it like that, don't substitute).
6. Work the dough until it makes "eyes", or air bubbles. Set aside.

To put the tamales together:

1. Take about three spoonsful of dough and place them on the center of a piece of banana leaf.
2. Dig a hole in the middle and place a piece of meat, a piece of egg, an olive, one peanut, and a wedge of the fresh aji Mirasol, this may be substituted by any fresh chile, although the aji Mirasol or aji amarillo (yellow chile) has a very distinctive flavor and is just mildly spicy.
3. Close the hole on the dough by adding a little bit more dough or folding and tapping it closed, pushing some of the surrounding dough on it.
4. Wrap well with the banana leaf, closing tightly all four sides on top of the dough. Use another piece of banana leaf to wrap the tamal again starting on the opposite direction and tie tightly using a string cut out of some more banana leaf or a common piece of string. Set aside.

5. Place the corn cobs at the bottom of a deep pot (rather big or medium size) and some of the banana leaves on top of the corn cobs.
6. Add just enough water to cover the leaves.
7. Place the tamales vertically and side by side so the steam travels freely through them and cover them with the rest of the banana leaves.
8. Cook for about 4 hours. Serve with a type of onion salad called salsa criolla.

Salsa Criolla:

1. Chop a whole onion julienne style, rinse once with water and salt, and pat dry.
2. Cut one or two small tomatoes in thin wedges.
3. Add two tablespoons of mint leaves, two tablespoons of cilantro leaves, and one fresh aji amarillo (yellow chile) deveined and sliced.
4. Toss everything together and add the juice of half a lime, freshly squeezed.
5. Season with salt and pepper to taste.
6. Serve each tamal warm, unwrapped, and with a couple of spoonsful of salsa criolla on top.
7. Decorate topping with a branch of parsley or cilantro. For Sunday breakfast place a roll of fresh french bread on the side of the dish.

Chapter Two: Peruvian Lunch Recipes

Peruvian Palta Rellena

Serves: 4

Ingredients:

- 2 avocados
- 2 cups cooked vegetables (I like to use cooked carrots, corn, peas, and raw tomato)
- 1 cup sunflower sprouts
- 1 lime
- ½ cup aioli (vegan garlic)
- salt and pepper to taste

Method:

1. First, cut the avocados in half and peel away the skin. Remove the pit. Take a spoon and hollow out a little more of the avocado halves to make the center a little bigger.
2. Sprinkle with a little of the lime juice and salt and pepper.
3. mixed the cooked vegetables and raw tomato with the Vegan Garlic Aioli in a bowl. Add salt and pepper to taste.
4. Place vegetable mixture inside of the hollowed out avocado halves. Top with sunflower sprouts.

Parihuela (Peruvian Seafood Soup)

Serves: 8

Ingredients:

- 1 plate-sized bream (about 600 g) cleaned and scored (or any seasonal fish, cut into 180 g pieces)
- 300 g baby calamari (cleaned and cut into 5 mm rings)
- 185 ml pale lager beer
- 60 ml (¼ cup) olive oil
- 16 mussels (cleaned)
- 8 pippies
- 8 scallops in the half shell
- 4 garlic cloves (minced)
- 2 onions (finely chopped)
- 1½ tablespoons aji Amarillo paste *(see note)*
- 1½ tablespoons aji Colorado paste *(see note)*
- 2 teaspoon corn flour (dissolved into a little cold water)
- 1 medium tomato (peeled, seeded and diced)
- plain flour (for dusting)
- salt and freshly ground white pepper to taste
- handful coriander sprigs and lime wedges (to serve)

For the stock:

- 1.5 kg fish heads and bones
- 150 ml dry white wine
- 4 green prawns
- 1 blue swimmer crab (cleaned and cut into quarters)
- 1 brown onion (roughly chopped)
- 1 bay leaf
- 1 carrot (roughly chopped)

- 1 celery stalk (roughly chopped)
- a squeeze of lemon juice
- handful fresh oregano and tarragon

Method:

1. *For the stock,* peel the prawns and reserve the shells. Remove the top shells of the crabs, then remove and discard the feathery gills and cut the bodies into quarters. Reserve the peeled prawns and crab bodies for later.
2. Place the prawn shells, crab shells and all the remaining ingredients into a large saucepan or stockpot.
3. Add 2 liters of water and bring to the boil over high heat. Reduce the heat to low and simmer for 20 minutes, skimming the impurities as it simmers. Strain the stock and discard the solids.
4. Return the stock to the pan and simmer until reduced by two-thirds. Strain again through a very fine strainer.
5. Dust the fish in flour and season with salt and white pepper. Heat half the oil in a frying pan over medium heat and gently lower in the fish. Fry for about 4 minutes on each side – you just want to cook it three-quarters of the way at this point. Remove from the pan and set aside.
6. Heat the remaining olive oil and garlic in a large wide frying pan over medium heat for 1-2 minutes or until aromatic. Add the onion and both the yellow and red chili pastes and cook for 5 minutes or until the onion begins to soften. Add the tomato and cook, stirring frequently for another 3 minutes or until aromatic. Add the crab pieces, beer and a ladle of the fish stock.
7. Add the fried bream and place the mussels and pippies around it. Gently bring to the boil and season with salt and white pepper. Cover and cook for 5 minutes. Add the scallops, prawns and baby calamari. Season again, cover and cook for a further 2 minutes.

8. Check for seasoning, add another ladle of stock - cover and cook for another 30 seconds.
9. Spoon the corn flour slurry into the liquid and gently shake the pan to thicken the sauce.
10. Garnish with coriander and serve with lime wedges.

Note:

- Aji Amarillo paste is made from dried yellow Peruvian chillies, while aji Colorado paste is made from dried red chillies. Both are available in jars from Latin delicatessens.

Grilled Peruvian Chicken Wraps

Serves: 4

Ingredients:

- 1 lb. boneless, skinless chicken breasts (cut in half)
- 5 garlic cloves (smashed)
- 2 tablespoons fresh lime juice
- 2 tablespoons ground cumin
- 1 tablespoon sweet smoky paprika
- 1 tablespoon 2% fat plain Greek yogurt
- ½ tablespoon dried oregano
- ½ tablespoon fresh ground black pepper
- 1/3 cup low-sodium soy sauce

Sauce:

- 4 high fiber flatbreads
- 2 tablespoons fresh lime juice
- 2 tablespoons reduced fat mayonnaise
- 2 tablespoons 2% fat plain Greek yogurt
- 1 jalapeno (roughly chopped)
- 1 garlic clove (smashed)
- 1 tablespoon apple cider vinegar
- ½ cup fresh packed cilantro (leaves and stems)
- pinch of salt
- lettuce, tomato, onion (optional)

Method:

1. First, puree the soy sauce through yogurt in a blender.
2. Pound chicken to uniform thickness.
3. Place the chicken into a large plastic bag and pour marinade over the chicken.

4. Close up the bag and massage the marinade into the chicken.
5. Refrigerate for 8 to 24 hours.
6. Heat your grill to medium-high heat with the coals on one side for indirect grilling. Oil the grates well.
7. Drain the chicken and pat dry with a paper towel.
8. Grill chicken about 4 minutes per side, or until done.

Sauce:

1. Place all ingredients into a blender and pulse until sauce is mostly pureed.
2. Slice chicken and place on flatbread.
3. Drizzle sauce.
4. Add lettuce, tomato and onion, if wanted.

Peruvian Avocado Tostada

Serves: 4

Ingredients:

- 4 Peruvian Avocados
- 4 small corn tortillas
- 3 green onions (roughly chopped)
- 1 lime (juiced)
- 1 lemon (juiced)
- 1 cup charred corn
- 1 cup halved heirloom cherry tomato
- ½ cup vegetable oil
- ½ cup shredded colby jack cheese
- salt and pepper to taste

For the cilantro vinaigrette:

- 2 cups (about 4 ounces) tightly packed fresh cilantro leaves, stems removed
- 2 tablespoons red wine vinegar
- 1 teaspoon salt
- 1 shallot (roughly chopped)
- 1 clove garlic
- ½ teaspoons red pepper flakes
- ½ cup olive oil

Method:

1. First, heat the oil over medium high heat in a pan or skillet until almost smoking. Add the tortillas into the oil, one at a time, and fry on each side for about 1-2 minutes until golden brown and crispy. Remove with tongs and

set aside to dry on a paper towel. Repeat process with other corn tortillas.

2. Cut the Peruvian avocados in half lengthwise. Remove the pit from the avocado and discard. Remove the avocado from the skin and place the avocado flesh into a bowl. Add the chopped green onions, lime juice, lemon juice and season with salt and pepper. Mash until half chunky and half smooth and then set aside.

3. Combine the corn and cherry tomatoes and top with 3 tablespoons of the cilantro vinaigrette.

To make the cilantro vinaigrette:

1. Combine all the ingredients for the vinaigrette in a high-powered blender and blend for 60 seconds until very smooth. Taste and adjust salt and pepper as needed

To assemble:

1. Slather equal parts of the avocado mixture on all of the fried tostadas. Top with equal parts of the tomato and corn mixture and a sprinkle of shredded cheese.

Quinua con Colinabo y Cebolla Perla (Quinoa with Kohlrabi and Pearl Onions)

Serves: 4

Ingredients:

- 240 g white quinoa
- 100 g trimmed purple kohlrabi (peeled and thinly sliced)
- 50 g baby onions (peeled but left whole)
- 20 g capers
- 3 tablespoons olive oil
- 1 cm piece of fresh root ginger (peeled and grated)
- handful of coriander and flat leaf parsley (chopped)
- salt and pepper to taste
- handful of borage flowers and young herbs (to garnish)

Method:

1. First, rinse the quinoa in cold running water until the water runs clear, then drain.
2. Place the quinoa in a saucepan with a tight-fitting lid and add water to cover by 5 cm. Cover with the lid and bring to the boil over a medium heat. Stir, re-cover and reduce the heat to low.
3. Cook for about 15 minutes – the quinoa is ready when you can see a little ring on the outside of the grain and it is soft. Rinse in cold water, then drain well.
4. Heat 1 tablespoon of the olive oil in a sauté pan and sauté the quinoa for 5 minutes. Set aside.
5. Heat another 1 tablespoon olive oil in a separate pan and sauté the onions until golden. Add the kohlrabi and capers.

6. Add the remaining tablespoon of olive oil to the first pan and sauté the grated ginger for 20 seconds. Add the sautéed quinoa and vegetables, and season with salt and pepper to taste, then stir in the chopped herbs.
7. Serve garnished with the borage flowers and young herbs.

Seitan Saltado (Peruvian Potato Stir-Fry)

Serves: 4

Ingredients:

- 1-pound russet potatoes (about 3 medium)
- 1-pound seitan
- 2 cloves garlic (minced or pressed)
- 2 tablespoons red wine vinegar
- 1 teaspoon ground cumin
- 1 medium-large red onion (sliced in wedges)
- 1 medium-large bell pepper (seeded and sliced)
- 1 jalapeno pepper (seeded and diced, adds heat–reduce if necessary)
- 1 medium-large tomato (chopped)
- 1 tablespoon soy sauce (or coconut aminos)
- 1/8 teaspoon ground black pepper
- ¼ cup parsley (minced)
- salt and pepper to taste

Method:

1. First, preheat the oven to 400° F. Line a baking sheet with parchment paper. Cut the potatoes into French fries, whatever size you like. (I used my mandolin to make skinny fries about 1/4-inch thick.)
2. Sprinkle the fries with salt and pepper and spread in a single layer on the baking sheet. Bake, turning every 10-15 minutes, until fries are browning and becoming crispy, about 40 minutes depending on the size of your fries. Keep warm.

3. While the fries are cooking, combine the seitan in a large bowl with the cumin, garlic, and a generous grinding of black pepper. Allow to marinate briefly while you prepare the other ingredients.

4. When the fries are almost done, heat a large non-stick wok or skillet. Sauté the red onion until it begins to soften, about 2 minutes. Add the bell and jalapeño peppers and cook another two minutes. Add the seitan and chopped tomato and cook, stirring, until hot throughout. Stir in the vinegar and soy sauce and gently fold in the French fries and parsley.

5. Serve alone or over rice with hot sauce on the side.

Pan Con Chicharron (Peruvian Pork Roll)

Serves: 6

Ingredients:

- 1 kg piece pork belly (skin on, scored)
- 6 French white rolls (halved)
- 1 tablespoon olive oil
- 1 sweet potato (kumera), peeled, cut into 8mm-thick slices
- vegetable oil (to shallow-fry)

Onion salsa:

- 2 tablespoons coriander leaves (finely chopped, plus extra leaves, to serve)
- 1 red onion (thinly sliced)
- 1 tablespoon lemon juice
- 1 tablespoon lime juice
- 1 bird's-eye chili (finely chopped)
- 1 tablespoon olive oil

Aji amarillo sauce:

- 200 g (⅔ cup) mayonnaise
- 2 tablespoon aji amarillo chilli paste *(see note)*
- 1 tablespoon lime juice

Method:

1. Start by preheating the oven to 160° C. Place pork belly in a roasting tray, rub 2 teaspoons of salt into skin and drizzle with oil. Place in oven and roast for 2 hours or until tender, then increase heat to 200°C and cook for a further 25 minutes or until skin is crisp. Set aside to rest.

2. *To make the salsa*, place onion in a bowl, cover with cold, salted water and set aside for 30 minutes. Drain then toss with remaining salsa ingredients.
3. Meanwhile, place sweet potato in a saucepan of cold, salted water and bring to the boil. Boil for 5 minutes or until just tender when pierced with a knife. Drain and cool, then pat dry with paper towel.
4. Heat 1 cm oil in a frying pan over medium heat. Working in batches, fry sweet potato for 4 minutes on each side or until golden.
5. *To make aji amarillo sauce*, combine all ingredients in a bowl and set aside.
6. Cut pork belly into thick pieces. Heat frying pan over medium heat and toast rolls on both sides, if desired. Spread bases with aioli then top with sweet potato slices, pork belly pieces, onion salsa, coriander and bun tops.

Note:

- Aji amarillo chilli paste is available from specialist food shops and delis.

Salchipapas (Peruvian Sausages and Potatoes)

Serves: 3

Ingredients:

- 4 beef hot dogs (or sausages)
- 2 russet potatoes
- vegetable oil (for frying)
- fresh parsley (chopped)
- ketchup
- mustard
- amarillo paste
- mayonnaise

Method:

1. First, fill a deep saucepan with at least 2 inches of the vegetable oil and place over medium heat. Cover a large plate with paper towels and set aside.
2. Peel and cut the potatoes into fries 1/3-1/2-inch-wide, then pat dry. Once the oil is heated to about 350 F, add the potatoes in batches. Fry until golden and transfer to the towel-lined plate.
3. In a large pan, drizzle about 1 teaspoon oil over medium heat. Thinly slice the hot dogs into ovals and add to the heated pan. Cook, stirring occasionally, until heated through and golden. Add the fried potatoes, tossing to combine.
4. Serve hot with a sprinkling of parsley and ketchup, mustard, aji amarillo, and mayonnaise for dipping.

Peruvian Crisp Potatoes Stuffed with Spiced Beef and Pecans

Serves: 4

Ingredients:

- 750 g sebago potatoes (peeled, chopped)
- 750 g beef brisket
- 500 ml (2 cups) beef stock
- 100 g (⅔ cup) raisins (chopped)
- 90 g (¾ cup) pecans (chopped)
- 80 ml (⅓ cup) vegetable oil
- 50 g (⅓ cup) plain flour
- 2 soft-boiled eggs
- 2 teaspoon ground cumin
- 2 garlic cloves (finely chopped)
- 1 small-medium onion (chopped)
- 1 teaspoon aji amarillo paste
- 1 teaspoon paprika
- 1 medium egg (lightly beaten)
- baby herbs *(see note),* to serve

Parsley and black olive topping:

- 160 g (1 cup) sun-dried black olives (seeded, finely chopped)
- 80 ml (⅓ cup) olive oil
- 1 cupflat-leaf parsley leaves (finely chopped)

Method:

1. First, place potatoes in a saucepan of cold water, bring to the boil and cook for 20 minutes or until tender. Drain.

Mash until smooth. Season with salt and pepper, then place in the fridge for 2 hours or until cold.

2. Meanwhile, place beef in a large pan with stock, onion, garlic, aji amarillo paste, spices, raisins, ½ tsp salt, ¼ tsp pepper and 500 ml water. Bring to the boil, then reduce heat to low, cover and cook for 1½ hours or until almost all the liquid has evaporated and beef is meltingly tender. Stir in pecans and cool for 30 minutes. Shred beef using 2 forks, then toss with juices and pecans. Set aside.

3. *To make the topping,* combine all the ingredients in a bowl. Season and set aside.

4. Stir beaten egg into the cold mashed potato until combined. Using floured hands, place 2 x ¼ cup mounds of mashed potato onto a sheet of baking paper. Flatten each mound to a 10 cm-patty. Place 1 potato patty in one hand and top with ¼ cup beef mixture. Place remaining potato patty on top and mould around beef into an oblong shape. Repeat with remaining mashed potato and beef mixture to make 4 stuffed potatoes.

5. Place flour in a shallow bowl and gently toss stuffed potatoes in flour to coat.

6. Cover the base of a large frying pan with baking paper, add 2 tbsp oil and heat over high heat. Add 2 stuffed potatoes and cook for 2 minutes each side or until golden. Repeat with remaining 2 tbsp oil and stuffed potatoes.

7. Cut stuffed potatoes in half and serve with half a soft-boiled egg, baby herbs and the parsley and black olive topping.

Ensalada Miraflores

Serves: 4

Ingredients:

- 1 (7 ounce/200 g) can butter beans (drained and rinsed)
- 7 ounces (200 g) queso fresco or feta cheese (cut into small cubes)
- 3 ½ ounces (100 g) bacon lardons
- 4 medium-large tomatoes (seeded and cut into 3/8-inch (1 cm) dice)
- 3 ears choclo or other corn
- 1 tablespoon olive oil
- 1 medium-large red onion (cut into 3/8-inch (1 cm) dice)
- 1 tablespoon flat-leaf parsley (finely chopped)
- ¼ rocoto chili (seeded and very finely chopped)

Dressing:

- 3 tablespoons extra virgin olive oil
- 3 tablespoons red wine vinegar
- a pinch of superfine sugar
- a squeeze of lime juice
- salt and freshly ground black pepper

Method:

1. First, bring a saucepan of water to a boil over medium heat and cook the choclo until tender. Drain and plunge into iced water to cool down and then cut or break off the kernels from the cob.

2. Heat the olive oil in a frying pan over medium heat and sauté the bacon lardons for a few minutes, until they are crisp and brown. Drain on paper towels.
3. Put the choclo, butter beans, onion, tomatoes, chili, and cheese in a large bowl.
4. Whisk all the dressing ingredients together in a small bowl or jug and pour into the bowl of salad. Gently toss everything together, trying not to break up the cheese.
5. Divide the salad among 4 shallow bowls and sprinkle over the bacon lardons and parsley.

Cebiche De Atun (Peruvian Canned Tuna Ceviche)

Serves: 2

Ingredients:

- (6 ounce) can solid white tuna packed in water
- 2 -3 tablespoons extra virgin olive oil
- 1 fresh jalapeno chili (seeded and minced)
- 1 small red onion (peeled and finely chopped)
- 1 ripe tomato (diced)
- 1 tablespoon fresh cilantro (chopped)
- ¼ cup fresh lime juice (1-2 limes)
- lettuce
- salt and pepper to taste
- fresh cilantro stem (for garnish)

Method:

1. Start by draining the tuna, invert it onto a small platter.
2. Sprinkle the chili and onion over the tuna and allow it to stand for a few minutes.
3. Then add the tomato, chopped cilantro, and salt and pepper to taste, and gently mix together.
4. Sprinkle the lime juice over all, and drizzle with the oil. Serve over lettuce if you like.
5. Garnish with sprigs of cilantro and serve.

Saltado De Vainitas

Serves: 6

Ingredients:

- 1 ¼ pounds chicken (cut into 1-inch cubes)
- 2 (12 ounce) packages frozen French-style green beans (thawed)
- 6 tablespoons soy sauce (divided)
- 4 roma (plum) tomatoes (cut into eighths)
- 3 tablespoons white wine vinegar
- 3 cloves garlic (minced)
- 2 chili peppers (seeded and diced)
- 1 tablespoon canola oil (divided)
- 1 tablespoon ground cumin (divided)
- 1 red onion (halved and sliced)
- 1 cup cilantro (chopped)
- salt to taste

Method:

1. Start by heating half the canola oil in a wok or large skillet over medium-high heat.
2. Sauté garlic and chili peppers in hot oil until fragrant, about 1 minute. Add chicken to the wok. Stir half the soy sauce and half the cumin into the chicken mixture; cook just until the chicken is no longer pink in the middle, 5 to 7 minutes.
3. Transfer mixture to a bowl, retaining some of the drippings in the skillet and return to heat.
4. Heat remaining oil in the skillet with the retained drippings. Stir onion with the remaining soy sauce and cumin into the oil mixture; cook and stir until the onion

is transparent, about 5 minutes. Add tomatoes to the onion mixture; cook and stir until the tomatoes begin to soften, about 1 minute.

5. Return chicken mixture to the wok; add green beans and vinegar. Cook and stir the mixture until the green beans are tender, about 10 minutes.

6. Season with salt and sprinkle cilantro over the mixture; toss to mix.

Papa Rellena (Peruvian Stuffed Potatoes)

Serves: 8-10

Ingredients:

- 2 lbs. medium-large potatoes
- 1 lb. soy meat (or ground beef)
- 2 hard-boiled eggs (peeled and chopped)
- 2 medium-large eggs
- 2 garlic cloves (minced)
- 1 onion (diced)
- 1 tablespoon tomato paste
- ½ cup raisins
- ½ cup black olives (sliced)
- ¼ cup vegetable oil
- salt and pepper to taste
- parsley (chopped)
- all-purpose flour
- 1 tablespoon ají panca paste (panca chili pepper paste that you can find in many stores or online, optional)

Method:

1. First, cook the potatoes in a saucepan with boiling water until they are tender (around 20 minutes, but it depends on the potato).
2. Peel them while hot, as fast as you can. Pass them through the ricer at once. Add salt and pepper. Keep covered while you cook the filling.
3. In a saucepan heat the oil over high heat, add the onion and garlic stirring, then the tomato paste and ají panca, if using. Add the soy meat (or ground beef), salt, pepper.

Stir and cover the saucepan. Cook over low heat for around 15 minutes, stirring every now and then.

4. Incorporate hard-boiled eggs, raisins, olives, and parsley. Turn off the heat.

5. With floured hands, knead the potatoes for a few seconds. Take a portion of the potato dough and flatten it between your hands. With a spoon put a portion of the soy filling in the center of the potato round. Close it with some extra potato dough and form a little "football".

6. Put the flour in a bowl, and mix the 2 extra eggs in another bowl. Roll every roll in the eggs, then in the flour, shaking the excess, and fry in a hot pan with hot oil until the potato forms a thin golden a crusty layer.

7. Move around every now and then to make sure every side becomes golden.

8. Drain over paper towel and serve immediately, with Salsa Criolla or plain rice.

Peruvian Ceviche

Serves: 4

Ingredients:

- 1 ½ pounds ono, mahimahi, or bluenose bass (diced)
- 4 butter lettuce leaves
- 1 orange sweet potato (such as Garnet or Jewel), boiled, peeled, and sliced
- 1 cob sweet corn (boiled and cut into 4 pieces)
- ¾ cup lime juice
- ½ small red onion (halved and slivered)
- ½ teaspoon salt
- ½ cup cilantro leaves (chopped)
- 1 tablespoon ají amarillo sauce (optional)
- 1 habanero chili (seeded, halved, and thinly sliced, optional)

Method:

1. First, rinse diced fish and slivered red onion in cold water and dry thoroughly.
2. In a large bowl, combine fish, red onion, lime juice, salt, habanero (if using), and ají amarillo sauce (if using). Cover and refrigerate 20 minutes.
3. Just before serving, stir in cilantro. Divide between 4 bowls and serve with sweet potato, corn, and lettuce leaves on the side.

Note:

- Ceviche is a national dish of Peru. Originally created by fishermen as a way to eat part of their catch during long days at sea, ceviche uses the acid in lime juice to "cook" the fish.

- *Ají Amarillo,* a yellow chili with a slightly sweet flavor and plenty of heat. Available in jars or as a puréed sauce at many Latin markets.

Cau Cau (Peruvian Tripe Stew)

Serves: 4

Ingredients:

For poaching tripe:

- 1 lb. beef honeycomb tripe (cleaned)
- 1-2 quarts water
- 2 sprigs fresh mint

For sofrito:

- 2 teaspoon garlic paste
- 2 tablespoons cooking oil
- 1 cup red onion (diced)
- ½ teaspoon aji amarillo paste
- ¼ teaspoon salt
- ¼ teaspoon oregano
- ¼ teaspoon turmeric
- ¼ teaspoon pepper
- ¼ teaspoon cumin

For stew:

- 1 lb. poached tripe (cut into 1" pieces)
- 1 lb. yellow potatoes (peeled and cut into 1" cubes)
- 2 cups tripe stock
- 2 teaspoons chicken bouillon paste
- 1 cup green peas
- mint (chopped, for garnish)

In addition to the ingredients above, you'll need one pot for poaching the tripe, and another for cooking the stew.

Method:

For poaching tripe:

1. First, place tripe into pot with enough water to cover.
2. Bring to a boil, and simmer for 30 minutes.
3. Remove from heat and discard water.
4. Add water again to cover the tripe, and add sprigs of mint.
5. Bring to a boil again, and simmer for 30 more minutes.
6. Remove tripe and set aside to cool, once cooled the tripe should be tender enough to tear by hand.
7. Save tripe stock, and strain mint.

For sofrito:

1. Heat cooking oil in a large pot over medium to high heat.
2. Add the garlic paste and diced onions.
3. Season with salt, pepper, cumin, oregano, and turmeric.
4. Add aji amarillo and sauté for a few minutes until onions are translucent.

For stew:

1. Cut the poached tripe into 1″ pieces.
2. Add the tripe pieces to the pot with the onion sofrito and mix well.
3. Add 1 cup of tripe stock, bring to a boil and simmer for 10 minutes.
4. Add the cubed potatoes, 1 more cup of tripe stock.
5. Mix well, taste stock and add chicken bouillon or adjust salt if needed.
6. Bring to a boil, and simmer for 20 more minutes, or until potatoes are cooked and the stock thickens.

7. Add the green peas, and continue to simmer for 5 more minutes.
8. Serve and garnish with chopped mint.

Notes:

- To make garlic paste, purée peeled garlic cloves with enough olive oil to create a smooth paste. Refrigerate the garlic paste in an airtight jar and use in a recipe as you would mince garlic.
- Aji amarillo is a very traditional Peruvian hot pepper with a savory flavor, yellow color, and lingering heat that is very important in this dish. You can pick up many Peruvian ingredients at Latino Markets.
- The challenge in cooking this dish is in finding the right balance of flavor between the tripe and all the other ingredients. If the tripe flavor is too strong, it may overwhelm the other savory components, that's why the water is changed during poaching. Conversely, if the tripe stock is mild after poaching, you can make it more savory by adding chicken bouillon when preparing the stew.

Arroz Tapado (Peruvian Meat-Filled Rice)

Serves: 6

Ingredients:

- 1 lb. ground beef
- 1 can (28 oz) organic tomatoes (diced)
- 3 cloves garlic
- 3 hardboiled eggs
- 2 teaspoons cumin
- 2 cups uncooked basmati rice
- 2 medium-large sweet potatoes
- 1 tablespoon smoked paprika
- 1 medium-large onion
- 1 green bell pepper
- ¼ cup parsley (chopped)
- ¼ cup black olives (chopped)

Method:

1. First, bring a large pot of water to a boil for the rice.
2. Chop the potatoes and toss in a small amount of olive oil and salt. Spread on a baking sheet and roast at 450°F until browned and tender.
3. Brown the meat and remove from the pan. Next, cook the onion and pepper for about 5 minutes. Add the garlic and spices and cook 2 minutes. Add the meat, tomatoes, eggs, parsley, and olives. simmer about 15 minutes, stirring often to mix well. Finally add the sweet potatoes and mix until heated through.
4. Boil the rice about 10 minutes until tender. Strain.
5. Depending on what size bowls you are using for a mold, the amount of rice and meat you use will vary. Spray the

inside of a bowl with nonstick spray and add rice to the bottom to about 1/3 of the way up the side.

6. Next, add the meat filling for the middle 1/3. Fill with rice to the top of the bowl and press down to make sure everything is tight.

7. Place a serving plate upside down onto the bowl, and flip the whole thing. Slowly remove the bowl and you should have a perfect mound of rice and beef.

Chapter Three: Peruvian Dinner Recipes

Aji de Gallina (Peruvian Spicy Creamed Chicken)

Serves: 4

Ingredients:

- 3 free-range chicken thighs (skin on, bone out)
- 750 g new potatoes
- 300 ml milk
- 125 g breadcrumbs
- 25 g Parmesan cheese
- 25 g shelled walnuts
- 2 cloves of garlic
- 1 large handful of black olives
- 1 onion
- olive oil
- a few sprigs of fresh mint
- 1–2 fresh red chilies (optional)
- ½ lemon (optional)

Method:

1. First, grind the walnuts in a pestle and mortar until fine. Halve and deseed the chilies, then pop into a blender with 100ml of water and blitz to a purée.
2. Boil the potatoes in a large pan of boiling salted water for about 15 minutes, or until cooked through. Drain and steam-dry in a colander for a few minutes, then return to the pan, dress with oil and season.

3. Put a lug of oil in a small frying pan over a medium heat. Destone and tear in the olives and pick in the mint leaves. Fry until lightly crispy, then add to the potatoes.

4. Place the chicken between 2 sheets of greaseproof paper and bash with a rolling pin or a heavy pan until flattened and an even thickness. Season well, drizzle with oil and place in the fridge until needed.

5. Peel and finely chop the onion and garlic, then gently fry in a non-stick pan over a low heat with a good lug of oil for 20 minutes, or until soft and sticky.

6. Stir in the blitzed chili and cook for a few more minutes before adding the breadcrumbs. Stir in the milk and cook for about 4 minutes, or until the sauce thickens, adding a splash of water, if needed.

7. Stir in the ground walnuts and finely grate in the Parmesan, simmer for a further 7 minutes, then season and keep warm while you cook the chicken.

8. Heat a griddle pan until screaming hot, then add the chicken, skin-side down. Cook for around 4 minutes, or until the skin is lovely and golden, then turn and cook on the other side for 3 to 4 minutes, or until cooked through.

9. Serve the chicken on the sauce with the potato salad on the side. Add a squeeze of lemon (if using) and some extra sliced chili, if you like.

Sancochado (Peruvian Braised Beef and Vegetables with Salsa Sauté)

Serves: 4

Ingredients:

- 2 lbs. beef short ribs
- 4 plum tomatoes diced (divided)
- 3 tablespoons olive oil
- 2 carrots (peeled and cut into 2-inch pieces)
- 2 corn on cobs (cut in half)
- 2 plantains (cut into 2-inch pieces)
- 2 garlic cloves (divided)
- 1 large spicy sausage (chorizo or cajun sausage)
- 1 large yellow onion (quartered)
- 1 chicken bouillon cube
- 1 tablespoon dried oregano
- 1 medium-large sweet potato (cut into large pieces)
- 1 medium yam (cut into large pieces)
- 1 red onion (diced)
- 1 orange bell pepper (diced)
- 1 red chili pepper (diced)
- 1 teaspoon white vinegar
- 1 teaspoon soy sauce
- 1 green onion (chopped)
- ½ cup cilantro (chopped)
- ½ head of cabbage (quartered)
- one lime (juiced)
- salt and freshly ground pepper to taste

Method:

1. First, set the oven rack to the bottom to allow for a large dutch oven or cast-iron pot. Preheat the oven to 400 F.

2. Place the short ribs, yellow onion, 1 garlic clove crushed, chicken bouillon, oregano, salt and freshly ground pepper in a large dutch oven or cast-iron pot. Pour water into the pot until the meat is about three quarters submerged.

3. Cover and bring the pot to a boil in on the stove top then transfer the dutch oven to the oven to braise the meat for 1 hour.

4. Remove the dutch oven from the oven. Add the carrots, sweet potato, yam, corn, plantain and cabbage to the pot. Add more water to the pot to submerge most of the ingredients (about ¾ of the pot).

5. Cover and bring the pot to a boil on the stove top then transfer the dutch oven to the oven to braise for another 45 minutes.

6. While the meat and root vegetables braise, heat the olive oil in a large skillet. Add the onions and 1 garlic clove minced to the pan and sauté over medium high heat for 1 minute.

7. Add the bell pepper, red chili pepper and 3 of the diced plum tomatoes and sauté until soft (about 5 minutes). Transfer the ingredients to a large bowl. Stir in the vinegar and soy sauce and let cool for 10 minutes. Once cool, add the remaining diced tomato, cilantro, green onion, and lime juice to the bowl. Stir the ingredients until well combined and set aside.

8. Remove the dutch oven from the oven. Using a large slotted spoon, place the meat, cabbage, corn, plantains and root vegetables on a large serving platter.

9. Serve the dish with sautéed salsa and cups or small bowls of the broth on the side. Enjoy.

Arroz Con Pollo (Chicken and Rice)

Serves: 5

Ingredients:

- 5 skinless chicken pieces
- 3 cups white rice
- 2 cups water
- 2 cloves garlic (minced)
- 1 tablespoon vegetable oil
- 1 medium-large onion (cut into small cubes)
- 1 cup fresh cilantro (chopped)
- 1 (12 fluid ounce) can beer
- 1 carrot (cut into small cubes)
- 1 cup green peas
- salt and ground black pepper to taste

Method:

1. First, heat vegetable oil in a heavy pot with a lid over medium heat. Season chicken with salt and pepper; cook in hot oil until just browned, about 2 minutes per side. Remove chicken to a platter, reserving drippings in the pot.
2. Sauté onion and garlic in the retained drippings until the onion is translucent, about 5 minutes. Stir cilantro into the onion mixture; season with salt and pepper. Cook and stir mixture for 2 minutes more.
3. Return chicken to the pot; add rice, water, beer, carrot, and peas. Place lid on the pot, reduce heat to low, and simmer until the rice absorbs the liquid completely and is tender, about 20 minutes.

Pollo Saltado (Peruvian-Style Chicken Stir-Fry)

Serves: 4

Ingredients:

- 2 large skinless, boneless chicken breast halves (cut into strips)
- ½ (32 ounce) package frozen steak-cut French fries
- 3 Roma tomatoes (sliced lengthwise and seeds removed)
- 2 tablespoons soy sauce
- 2 tablespoons vinegar
- 1 teaspoon paprika
- 1 teaspoon ground cumin
- 1 clove garlic (minced)
- 1 onion (sliced lengthwise)
- 1 green bell pepper (sliced into strips)
- 1 aji pepper (minced)
- ½ tablespoon vegetable oil
- ground black pepper to taste

Method:

1. First, place chicken strips in a resealable plastic bag with soy sauce, vinegar, paprika, cumin, black pepper, and garlic. Seal bag and shake up to cover chicken completely. Let marinate in the refrigerator for at least 15 minutes and as long as 24 hours.
2. Preheat the oven to 450 degrees F (230 degrees C). Arrange frozen fries in a single layer on a baking sheet.
3. Bake in the preheated oven until light golden, about 20-25 minutes.

4. In the meantime, heat oil in a large wok on high heat. Add the marinated chicken. Cook, flipping pieces occasionally, until mostly white on the surface, 4 to 5 minutes.
5. Add onion, bell pepper, and aji pepper to the wok with the chicken. Continue stir-frying until onions are slightly translucent but still hold their shape, 3 to 5 minutes.
6. Arrange baked fries on plates and place the chicken stir-fry on top.

Note:

- Use any color bell pepper you prefer. Feel free to substitute aji pepper with another kind of chile pepper or chile pepper past.

Arroz Chaufa (Peruvian Fried Rice)

Serves: 4

Ingredients:

- 2 cups boneless, skinless, chicken thighs
- 2 ½ cups cooked white rice (cold, Cook the rice in chicken broth or chicken base like Better than Bouillon instead of water)
- 1/2-inch chicken breast
- 5 medium-large eggs (scrambled and then roughly chopped)
- 3 tablespoons vegetable oil
- 2 garlic cloves (minced)
- 2 pinches cumin
- 1 whole red bell pepper (diced)
- 1 pinch sugar
- ½ cup onions (diced small)
- ½ cup sliced green onions (thinly, plus the white parts)
- ¼ teaspoon sesame oil
- ¼ teaspoon ground ginger (only add it if you are not using fresh ginger, if using fresh, use 1 tablespoon and cook it with the fresh veggies)
- 1/8 cup soy sauce
- salt and pepper to taste
- sauce mix

Method:

1. First, heat the oil in a large skillet over medium high heat.
2. Add the red bell peppers and onions. Sauté until softened, about 6 minutes. Right before the peppers and

onions are done add the fresh ginger (if using fresh ginger) and green onions, sauté for a min. Add the chicken and carefully mix well and cook for a couple minutes or until cooked through.

3. Add half the rice. Mix well then add the rest of the rice. Mix well. Add the soy sauce mixture. Mix well then add the chopped scrambled eggs. Toss.
4. Season with salt and pepper.
5. Serve while warm.

Note:

- This recipe moves pretty fast so get all of your veggies diced and minces and in order.
- Skinless chicken thighs is the preferred choice. They are full of flavor and they will taste amazing in this dish. If all you have is chicken breast, feel free do use that too.
- If you want to save time, use prepackaged already diced peppers, garlic and onion.
- Mix all these ingredients together in a small bowl: Soy sauce, sesame oil, a pinch or two of sugar, couple pinches of cumin, ground ginger. If you prefer to use fresh add 1 tablespoon. Do not add fresh ginger into the soy sauce mixture. We will be cooking the ginger with the rest of the veggies.

Sopa Criolla (Peruvian Beef Noodle Soup)

Serves: 10

Ingredients:

- 2 pounds beef stew meat (cut into 1/2-inch cubes)
- 1/2-pound zucchini (halved lengthwise and cut in 1/4-inch slices)
- 8 cups beef broth
- 2 ½ cups 1/4-inch pieces carrot
- 1 (8 ounce) package fideo pasta
- 4 cloves garlic (minced)
- 2 tablespoons tomato paste
- 2 bay leaves
- 2 tablespoons olive oil
- 2 cups Spanish onion (diced)
- 1 teaspoon dried oregano
- 1 pinch kosher salt to taste
- 1 pinch ground black pepper to taste

Method:

1. Start by heating the oil in a 5-quart pot over medium heat. Cook about half the beef in hot oil until completely browned, about 5 minutes. Remove beef with a slotted spoon to a bowl. Repeat with remaining beef.
2. Cook and stir onion and garlic in the oil remaining in the pot until the onion is soft, about 4 minutes. Return beef to the pot; add tomato paste and stir to coat beef in paste.
3. Stir oregano and bay leaves into the beef mixture; season with kosher salt and pepper. Cook and stir the mixture just until the oregano is fragrant, about 1 minute.

4. Pour beef broth into the pot, cover the pot, and bring the broth to a boil. Reduce heat to medium-low and simmer liquid until the beef is very tender, about 90 minutes.

5. Bring a large pot of lightly salted water to a boil. Cook fideo in the boiling water, stirring occasionally until cooked through but firm to the bite, 4 to 5 minutes. Drain.

6. Stir carrot and zucchini into the liquid; cook until the carrots are tender, about 15 minutes. Remove and discard bay leaves. Season again with kosher salt and pepper. Stir fideo into the broth; cook until the noodles are hot, about 1 minute.

Sudado de Pescado Criollo (Peruvian Steamed Fish)

Serves: 4

Ingredients:

- 1 lb. true cod fillet (cut into 4 pieces)
- 8 ginger rounds (peeled)
- 4 tablespoons cooking oil
- 2 garlic cloves (minced)
- 2 teaspoons aji amarillo paste
- 2 cups fish stock (prepared ahead of time)
- 2 limes (juiced)
- 1 roma tomato (cut into 8 wedges)
- ½ red onion (peeled and cut into feathers)
- ½ red bell pepper (julienned)
- ½ cup sweet peas
- ¼ cup dry white wine
- cooked sweet potatoes (peeled and cut into 8 rounds)
- cilantro and green onions for garnish
- salt, pepper, cumin, and oregano to taste
- *In addition to the ingredients above, you'll need a large pan with cover.*

Method:

1. First, sauté the red onions and red peppers in a pan with cooking oil over medium to high heat, add the garlic, aji amarillo paste, and mix well.
2. Add the tomatoes, and season with salt, pepper, cumin, and oregano, continue to mix.
3. Add the fish stock, half the lime juice, ginger rounds, and bring to a boil.

4. Place the fish fillets in the pan, add the white wine, reduce to a simmer and cover for about 10 minutes.
5. Add the sweet peas a few minutes before the fish is done.
6. Remove from heat, keep covered, and let sit for a few minutes.
7. Uncover, drizzle the rest of the lime juice over the fish, and garnish with sweet potato rounds, cilantro, and green onions.
8. Serve family-style with a side of steamed white rice, a seasonal green salad, and white wine.

Notes:

- I used a 12″ Paella pan and covered it with a half baking sheet.
- For the fish stock, I used Better Than Bouillon fish base paste at half strength, that is 1 teaspoon of paste for 2 cups of water. Sauté the red onions, red pepper, and tomatoes for a short time only, they should remain fairly crisp before adding the fish stock. Seasoning is to taste, but you can add 2-3 pinches of each spice, or about ¼ teaspoon.
- Add only 1 cup of the fish stock to the pan at first, there should be enough stock to create steam but the fish should not be covered by the stock. After placing the fish in the pan, ladle some of the onions, red peppers, and stock over the fish. While the fish is cooking, check the level of the stock and add more if needed.
- To test for doneness, carefully uncover the pan, and use a spoon to break off a piece of the fish, it should break off easily with little effort.
- The green onions can be julienned or chopped for garnish.

Salmon Tartare Peruvian Style

Serves: 2

Ingredients:

- 300 grams salmon (boneless and skinless)
- 4 cherry tomatoes (chopped)
- 2 limes juice
- 1 teaspoon coriander (finely chopped)
- 1 tablespoon Worcestershire sauce
- 1 teaspoon soy sauce
- 1 tablespoon olive oil
- ½ avocado
- ½ teaspoon mustard
- salt
- white pepper

Method:

1. First, cut the skinless salmon into small cubes. *(see note 1)*
2. Prepare the marinate mixing the soy sauce, the Worcestershire sauce, the mustard, the lime juice and the olive oil.
3. Pour the mix into the salmon. Add the coriander, the tomatoes, a pinch of salt and pepper. Stir and let it rest for 10 minutes.
4. Serve with the help of a round small vessel (you can use a glass). Put a layer of the marinated salmon, then a layer of chopped avocado and finally one of salmon. *(see note 2)*
5. Garnish with fresh coriander. Serve along with small toasts with a bit of balsamic glass.

Note:

- Cut the salmon in pieces of 1 cm (about half an inch, or even smaller). If you cut too small pieces these will mince, and if the pieces are too big, they will not get "cooked" by the lime.
- Try to squish the excess juice to help the tartare be more compact.

Seco de Cordero (Peruvian Lamb Stew)

Serves: 8

Ingredients:

- 2 lb. boneless leg of lamb
- 4 medium-large carrots
- 2 cups beef stock
- 2 medium-large yellow potatoes
- 4 cloves of garlic
- 1 red onion
- 1 teaspoon aji amarillo
- 1 bunch of cilantros
- ¼ cup green peas
- salt, pepper, cumin, oregano to taste
- canola oil
- *In addition to the ingredients above, you'll need a large pot to cook the lamb and an immersion blender to make the cilantro purée.*

Method:

1. First, mince the garlic and dice the onion, potatoes, and carrots. Remove the cilantro leaves from the bunch and purée in ½ cup of water. Cut the lamb into bite size pieces. Prepare the beef stock.
2. Season the lamb with salt and pepper and brown in a pot with canola oil over medium to high heat. Work in batches if necessary. Remove the lamb from the pot when done.
3. In the same pot, add some more canola oil and sauté the onions, garlic, and aji amarillo sofrito over medium heat. Season with cumin and oregano to taste.

4. Add ½ of the cilantro purée to the sofrito to deglaze the pot.
5. Return the lamb to the pot, add 1 cup of the beef stock, and reduce heat to a simmer for 30 minutes.
6. Add the remainder of the cilantro purée, ½ cup of stock, potatoes, carrots and continue to simmer for another 30 minutes.
7. Add the green peas and turn off heat, mix well.
8. Serve warm with a side of steamed rice and frejoles.

Note:

- To make the beef stock, I used one teaspoon of Better than Bouillon Beef Base to 1 cup of water. And though I made 2 cups of stock, I only used the sufficient amount to add to the sauce that was reduced while slow cooking.

Peruvian Seafood Soup

Serves: 5

Ingredients:

- 1-pound white fish
- 1-pound medium shrimp
- 1-pound red potatoes (little, large diced)
- 900 milliliters fish stock
- 2 cloves garlic (minced)
- 2 jalapeno peppers (seeds and veins removed and minced)
- 2 sprigs fresh thyme (or ½ tsp. dried thyme)
- 1 lime
- 1 tablespoon canola oil
- 1 medium onion (diced)
- ¼ cup cilantro (chopped)
- salt to taste
- seabass

Method:

1. Heat the canola oil over medium heat in a large saucepan and add the onion and cook until translucent about 5-7 min.
2. Stir in garlic and jalapenos and cook for about 1 min. Add the potatoes, fish stock, salt, and thyme sprigs. Bring up to boil and then reduce to a simmer and cook for 10 min.
3. Cut lime in half and the other half into 4 wedges, set aside. Add the lime half and fish to the soup. Cover and cook for 5 min. Add the shrimp and continue to cook for 3-5 min. more or just until shrimp are opaque and cooked through.

4. Remove the lime half and squeeze the juice into the soup.
5. Sprinkle each serving with cilantro and serve with a lime wedge.

The Hirshon Peruvian Ceviche

Serves: 4

Ingredients:

- 1 ½ pounds sea bass fillets (or use flounder, fluke or snapper cut into 1-inch pieces)
- 1/2-pound sweet potatoes (peeled and cut into 1-inch thick slices)
- 1/2-pound purple potatoes (peeled and cut into 1-inch thick slices, substitute Yukon Gold, if you can't find the purple ones)
- 5 cloves garlic (crushed through a press)
- 3 ears fresh corn (cleaned and cut into 2-inch thick slices)
- 2 chilis (rocoto, seeds and stems removed, cut into rings, available at Latin American markets or substitute thin rings of serrano peppers)
- 2 pepper (Aji amarillo, ground to a paste, available at Latin American markets or 1 tablespoon Aji pepper paste from the jar)
- 1 ½ cups fresh lime juice
- 1 teaspoon paprika
- 1 medium-large red onion (thinly sliced)
- 1 teaspoon salt
- ¼ teaspoon ground white pepper (freshly)
- ¼ cup cilantro leaves (minced)
- ¼ cup lemon juice
- ¼ cup grapefruit juice (note – this lime/lemon/grapefruit juice combo is a replacement for bitter orange juice – if you can find them, use 2 cups of that juice instead)

- lettuce leaves (bibb)

Method:

1. First, place the cut and cleaned fish into a large non-metal bowl and sprinkle with salt, pepper and the garlic/Aji pepper paste – toss well and let sit for at least 30 minutes.
2. Add ½ of the rocoto chili rings, paprika, onion, cilantro, juice and mix lightly; cover the mixture and refrigerate for 3 to 5 hours – make sure the flesh is opaque, meaning the acids have thoroughly 'cooked' the fish.
3. About 30 minutes before serving the fish, broil the sweet potatoes until lightly browned – turn them and remove when other side is also lightly browned (Suggestion from a Peruvian friend); Simultaneously, put up a pot of boiling water and add the corn to pot and cook for 10 minutes, or until tender. Drain and reserve, at room temperature, for the garnish.
4. Drain the fish thoroughly in a colander and arrange the Bibb lettuce leaves on 4 dinner plates.
5. Place the fish on the lettuce leaves and garnish with the reserved chili rings and surround the fish with the cooked potatoes and corn.

Grilled Peruvian Chicken

Serves: 6

Ingredients:

- 5 chicken legs
- 5 garlic cloves (minced)
- 4-5 bone in skin on chicken thighs
- 3 tablespoons fresh lime juice
- 2 teaspoons ground cumin
- 2 tablespoon vegetable oil
- 1 teaspoon smoked paprika
- ½ cup soy sauce
- ½ teaspoon dried oregano
- lime wedges

Method:

1. Whisk together the soy sauce, lime juice, garlic, cumin, paprika, dried oregano, and vegetable oil in a bowl. Pour it into a zip top back and add in all of the chicken pieces. Seal the bag and marinade chicken for 8 hours or overnight.
2. At least one hour prior to grilling, remove the chicken from the fridge and allow it to come to room temperature – to take the chill off the bone and promote better cooking.
3. Preheat the grill (we used gas), over high heat, and then reduce to medium for cooking. Place the chicken skin side down and grill for about 10 minutes, and then flip to other side. Rotate chicken to other areas of the grill if you find some pieces getting done too quickly.

4. Continue to cook for 10-15 minutes, or until the chicken registers at 165 degrees with an instant read thermometer. Be sure to not hit the bone when taking the temperature or you will get a false reading. Let the chicken rest at least 5 minutes prior to serving.
5. Serve with additional lime wedges for spritzing when serving.

Pachamanca a la Olla

Serves: 6

Ingredients:

For pachamanca marinade:

- 4 teaspoons garlic paste
- 2 teaspoons aji panca paste
- 3 teaspoons red wine vinegar
- ½ cup parsley leafs
- ½ cup cooking oil
- ½ cup mint leafs
- ½ cup cilantro leafs
- ½ teaspoon salt
- ½ teaspoon pepper
- ½ teaspoon cumin
- ½ teaspoon oregano

Ingredients for meat:

- 3 chicken thighs (skin and bone on)
- ¾ lb. pork shoulder (cut into 3 pieces)

Ingredients for vegetables:

- 3 medium-large potatoes (about 1 lb.), cut in halves
- 2 medium-large sweet potatoes (about 1 lb.), cut in thirds
- 1 ½ cups cooked hominy

Ingredients for bouquets:

- 12 mint sprigs
- 12 cilantro sprigs

- 12 parsley sprigs

Additional ingredients:

- 24 corn husks, or enough for 4 layers of corn husks
- 4-6 tablespoons cooking oil for searing meat
- 1 ½ cups vegetable stock

In addition to the ingredients above, you'll need a tall pot with a lid, parchment paper to seal the top of the pot, and string to tie the bouquets.

Method:

1. First, purée all the marinade ingredients using an immersion blender, and divide into two equal parts.
2. Place all the meat in a container, cover the chicken and pork pieces with half the marinade, seal the container, and refrigerate for 2 hours.
3. Place the pot lid over a piece of parchment paper, and cut a circle of parchment paper with a radius that is 1″ larger than the radius of the lid.
4. Make 3 herb bouquets tied with strings, each bouquet has 4 mint sprigs, 4 cilantro sprigs, and 4 parsley sprigs.
5. Sear the chicken in a skillet with oil over medium to high heat.
6. Sear the pork in a skillet with oil over medium to high heat.
7. Cover the bottom of the pot with corn husks, arrange the pork in one layer, place one herb bouquet with the pork, and cover the pork with corn husks.
8. Arrange the chicken in a second layer, place one herb bouquet with the chicken, and cover the chicken with corn husks.
9. Arrange the potatoes, sweet potatoes, and hominy in a third layer, brush the remaining marinade over the

vegetables, place one herb bouquet with the vegetables, and cover the vegetables with corn husks.

10. Pour the vegetable stock down the sides of the pot so that it collects in the bottom of the pot, cover the pot with the round piece of parchment paper, and place the lid on the pot.

11. Turn on heat to low, and cook for 1 hour, until meat is cooked through and vegetables are tender.

12. Give thanks to Pachamama before opening the pot and serving the Pachamanca.

Notes:

- *To make garlic paste,* purée peeled garlic cloves with enough olive oil to create a smooth paste. Refrigerate the garlic paste in an airtight jar and use in a recipe as you would mince garlic.

- Aji panca is a very traditional Peruvian hot pepper with an earthy color and smoky flavor that is very important in this dish. You can pick up many Peruvian ingredients at Latino Markets.

- For the vegetable stock, I used Better than Bouillon Vegetable Base paste.

- For each layer of corn husks, I used 6 pieces, 3 pieces arranged in parallel, and the other 3 pieces arranged transversely to the first 3 pieces, creating a uniform and tightly packed layer of corn husks. The first layer of corn husks is arranged on the bottom of the pot, the second layer over the pork, the third layer over the chicken, and the fourth layer over the vegetables.

Tallarines Verdes (Peruvian-Style Pesto)

Serves: 4

Ingredients:

- 1-pound spaghetti
- 4 cups spinach leaves
- 2 garlic cloves (finely diced)
- 1 cup basil leaves
- 1 cup green beans (cooked)
- 1 tablespoon olive oil
- ¾ cup evaporated milk
- ½ cup parmesan cheese (grated)
- ½ cup fresh cheese (white, queso fresco, diced in cubes)
- ¼ cup pecans
- ¼ cup red onion (diced)
- ¼ cup olive oil
- salt and pepper to taste

Method:

1. First, cook the pasta in boiling salted water following the package instructions.
2. Meanwhile sauté the onion in 1 tablespoon oil, at medium heat and stirring occasionally, until translucent (about 10 minutes).
3. Pour boiling water over the spinach and basil leaves (you can use the same water for the pasta). Strain.
4. In the blender process onion, spinach, basil, garlic, evaporated milk, white cheese, pecans, olive oil, salt and pepper.

5. Drain the pasta and mix with the sauce and the green beans.
6. Serve immediately, sprinkled with Parmesan cheese.

Peruvian Sopa Seca

Serves: 4

Ingredients:

- 2 pounds bone-in chicken breast
- 500 grams linguini or spaghetti (broken in half)
- 4 cups chicken broth
- 2 tablespoons parsley (minced)
- 2 tablespoons oil
- 2 aji amarillo peppers (Julienned)
- 2 tablespoons onion (finely diced)
- 1 teaspoon salt
- 1 cup fresh butter beans
- 1 tablespoon garlic (minced)
- 1 tablespoon aji panca paste
- ½ teaspoon sugar
- ½ cup finely diced tomato (peeled and deseeded)
- ¼ cup basil puree
- freshly ground black pepper

Method:

1. In a medium saucepan, cover chicken with water and bring to a boil over high heat. Reduce heat to a simmer and cook over low heat for 20 minutes. Remove from heat, drain and reserve chicken.
2. In a deep sauté pan, heat oil over medium high heat. Add onion, salt and sugar. Sauté until golden in color, about 5 minutes. To the onions, add tomato, basil puree, aji panca paste and black pepper.
3. Sauté for 2 more minutes, stirring to combine.

4. Add the aji amarillo peppers, butter beans and parsley to the mixture, stirring to coat. Add in dry noodles and broth, stirring gently to coat with sauce.
5. Turn heat down to a low heat, cover, and simmer for 10 to 12 minutes or until broth has just been absorbed. Remove from heat.

Carapulcra (Freeze Dried Potatoes with Pork)

Serves: 4

Ingredients:

- 1 lb. (400 g) freeze dried potatoes
- 2 lb. (1 k) boneless pork meat
- 3 ½ oz (100 g) peanuts (toasted and coarsely processed)
- 4 cups chicken bouillon
- 3 tablespoons ají panca molido or sundried red aji (chili) paste
- 3 crackers
- 2 tablespoons (50 g) crushed garlic
- 2 tablespoons ají mirasol or sundried yellow aji (chili) paste
- 1 cup dry white wine
- 1 tablespoon cumin
- ½ teaspoon pepper
- ¼ cup red vinegar
- ¼ cup port wine
- salt

Method:

1. First, brown freeze-dried potato in a skillet until golden. Transfer to a bowl and cover with water for 30 minutes approximately.
2. Cut ¾ of pork meat in large pieces and the rest in small pieces.
3. Marinate meat in a mixture of vinegar, pepper, cumin, white wine, ají, garlic and salt.

4. Fry pieces of meat (large ones) in ½ cup oil. Remove meat.
5. Fry small pieces in same oil.
6. Pour oil left from meat in another pan. Add ½ cup more. Pour marinade and cook for 2 minutes.
7. Add bouillion and freeze-dried potato drained. Mix.
8. Reduce heat and cook for 1 ½ hours stirring frequently. Add meat pieces and cook for another ½ hour until well done.
9. Before removing from heat, add toasted peanuts processed with crackers, and port wine.
10. Serve with white rice.

Escabeche de Pescado (Peruvian Pickled Fish)

Serves: 4

Ingredients:

For the fish:

- 1 lb. cod
- 2-4 tablespoons cooking oil
- ½ cup flour
- salt and pepper to taste

For pickling sauce:

- 4 teaspoons honey
- 4 teaspoons red wine vinegar
- 2-4 tablespoons olive oil
- 2 cups fish stock
- 1 bay leaf
- 1 teaspoon garlic paste
- 1 teaspoon aji panca
- 1 red onion (sliced into feathers)
- ¼ teaspoon salt
- ¼ teaspoon pepper
- ¼ teaspoon cumin
- ¼ teaspoon oregano

Ingredients for garnish:

- 8 lettuce leaves
- 4 Kalamata olives
- 1 sweet potato (peeled, cooked, cut into rounds)
- 1 habanero pepper (julienned)
- 1 medium egg (hard boiled, cut into quarters)

In addition to the ingredients above, you'll need pots to cook the sweet potato and hardboiled egg, a skillet for the fish, a sauce pan for the pickling sauce, and a deep dish for letting the fish sit in the pickling sauce before serving.

Method:

Preparation for fish:

1. First, clean and cut the fish into 4 pieces, season with salt and pepper.
2. Coat each piece of fish with flour, shake off excess flour, and pan fry the fish in a skillet with 2-4 tablespoons cooking oil over medium to high heat.
3. Cook each piece until it's a golden brown, about 4 minutes per side, or until fish is cooked through.
4. After cooking the fish, transfer the pieces to a deep dish and set aside.

Preparation for pickling sauce:

1. Heat olive oil in a sauté pan over medium heat.
2. Sauté the onion, garlic paste, and aji panca for a few minutes.
3. Season with salt, pepper, cumin, and oregano.
4. Add the fish stock, and mix in the honey and red wine vinegar.
5. Add the bay leaf, reduce heat, and simmer for 10-15 minutes.
6. Remove from heat, and let cool to room temperature.

Preparation for escabeche:

1. Pour picking sauce over fish in dish.

2. Toss the onions to mix well.
3. Let rest for one hour before serving at room temperature.
4. Periodically scoop sauce over fish.
5. Plate individual servings of fish over a bed of lettuce with cooked sweet potato rounds, scoop the sauce with onions over the fish, and garnish with hardboiled egg quarters and Kalamata olives.

Notes:

- To make garlic paste, purée peeled garlic cloves with enough olive oil to create a smooth paste. Refrigerate the garlic paste in an airtight jar and use in a recipe as you would mince garlic.
- Aji panca is a very traditional Peruvian hot pepper with an earthy color and smoky flavor that is very important in this dish. You can pick up many Peruvian ingredients at Latino Markets.
- The key to the pickling sauce is to find the balance between spicy, sweet, and sour flavors. Use a light honey that has mild aromatics that won't overwhelm the other flavors in the sauce. Use equal parts honey and red wine vinegar but taste the sauce and adjust if needed.

Peruvian Chicken Stew

Serves: 4

Ingredients:

- 1-pound boneless (skinless chicken thighs)
- ¾ pound all potato purpose (cut into 1/2-inch chunks)
- 2 cloves garlic (finely chopped)
- 2 tablespoons country crock spread
- 1 onion (medium, chopped)
- 1 chicken flavor bouillon
- 1 teaspoon habanero chili pepper
- ½ teaspoon ground cumin
- ½ cup water
- ¼ cup peanut butter

Method:

1. You can start by seasoning the chicken, if desired, with salt and ground black pepper. In 12-inch skillet, heat olive oil over medium-high heat and brown chicken. Remove chicken and set aside. Reserve 1 tablespoon drippings.
2. Add potatoes, onion and cumin to reserved drippings and cook, stirring occasionally, 5 minutes. Reduce heat to medium and cook garlic and habanero chili pepper sauce 30 seconds, stirring frequently. With wire whisk, whisk in peanut butter blended with water and chicken flavor bouillon, stirring until smooth.
3. Return chicken to skillet. Simmer covered 30 minutes or until potatoes are tender and chicken is thoroughly cooked.

4. Serve, if desired, with hot cooked rice.

Pollo a la Brasa (Peruvian Grilled Chicken)

Serves: 4

Ingredients:

Aji verde:

- 5 jalapenos (seeds removed, if you don't like spice also remove veins)
- 1 cup cilantro
- 1 small-medium yellow onion
- 1 tablespoon lime juice
- 1 medium-large garlic clove
- 1/3 cup feta cheese or queso fresco
- 1/3 cup canola oil
- kosher salt to taste

Aji amarillo:

- 1 small yellow onion
- 1 large garlic clove
- 1 tablespoon lime juice
- ½ teaspoon huacatay paste
- 1/3 cup feta cheese or queso fresco
- ¼ cup ají amarillo paste
- ¼ cup canola oil
- kosher salt to taste

Peruvian chicken:

- 3 lb. chicken (fresh or defrosted)
- 4 tablespoons canola oil
- 3 tablespoons paprika
- 2 tablespoons ground cumin

- 2 tablespoons lime juice
- 1.5 tablespoons garlic (minced)
- 1 teaspoon freshly ground black pepper
- ½ teaspoon kosher salt
- ½ cup water to add to Instant Pot only
- ¼ cup cilantro (chopped, for garnish)

Method:

Aji verde:

1. First, place everything but oil and salt in blender and pulse to chop. Stream in canola oil until it's blended smoothly. As some feta is saltier than others taste for seasoning and add kosher salt as needed.

Aji amarillo:

1. First, place everything but oil and salt in blender and pulse to chop. Stream in canola oil until it's blended smoothly. As some feta is saltier than others taste for seasoning and add kosher salt as needed.

Oven roasted peruvian chicken:

1. Marinate chicken in spice mixture for one hour, or ideally overnight.
2. Preheat oven to 350 F.
3. Place dutch oven on stove over medium-high heat. Heat 2 tablespoons of canola oil until it shimmers. Brown chicken on all sides.
4. Cook in oven with lid on for 80 minutes. Remove lid and cook for another 10-20 minutes. Internal temperature should be 165 F.

Instant pot peruvian chicken:

1. Marinate chicken in spice mixture for one hour, or ideally overnight.
2. Turn Instant Pot on sauté and heat 2 tablespoons of canola oil until it shimmers. Brown chicken on all sides.
3. Remove chicken. Add ½ cup water to the Instant Pot and place chicken on trivet in pot.
4. Cook on manual setting and cook 6 minutes per pound, or 18 minutes for a 3lb chicken. NPR (natural pressure release) for 10 minutes.
5. Garnish with chopped parsley and serve alongside fries and aji amarillo and verde.

Peruvian Cilantro Rice

Serves: 6

Ingredients:

- 2 (4 ounce) skinless boneless chicken breast (halves)
- 1 cup white rice (uncooked)
- 1 tablespoon garlic (minced)
- 1 tablespoon cumin
- 1 bunch cilantro stems (fresh, removed)
- 1 tablespoon vegetable oil
- ½ cup water
- ¼ cup carrots (frozen, chopped)
- salt and pepper to taste
- ¼ cup frozen peas (optional)

Method:

1. First, place the chicken into a large saucepan and fill with enough water to cover, about 3 cups.
2. Bring to a boil and cook for about fifteen minutes, or until chicken is done. Dice chicken, and reserve cooking liquid.
3. In a food processor or blender, puree cilantro with ½ cup water.
4. Heat oil in a saucepan and cook garlic until lightly browned. Pour in 2 cups of the cooking liquid and stir in the cilantro puree, diced chicken, carrots, peas, cumin and rice.
5. Season with salt and pepper to taste. Bring to a simmer, then cover; cook on low heat until rice is tender and liquid has been absorbed, 15 to 20 minutes.

Ocopa Con Camarones (Shrimp in Ocopa Sauce)

Serves: 8

Ingredients:

- 2.2 lb. (1 k) shrimp
- 7 oz ¼ lb. (200 g) ají mirasol / sundried yellow aji (chili)
- 12 nuts (any to your liking)
- 10 graham crackers
- 1 ½ cup boiled water
- 1 garlic clove
- ¾ cup olive oil
- ½ medium-size onion (coarsely cut)
- ½ key lime
- oil (necessary quantity)
- salt and pepper to taste

Method:

1. First, cut, seed and devein aji, using gloves. Wash thoroughly with water, rubbing insides one against the other.
2. Place aji, onion and garlic on baking sheet and take to oven 350° F (175° C) until golden.
3. Shell and devein shrimps. Set tails aside.
4. Fry shrimp heads, claws and shells in ½ cup olive oil. Liquefy this in blender with 1 ½ cup boiled water. Strain. Reserve liquid.
5. Remove aji from baking sheet and place in bowl. Cover with water just boiled for 4 or 5 hours. This process will take hotness from aji. Discard water.
6. Blend or process aji, onion, garlic, nuts, and graham crackers with the reserved liquid from shrim. While

blending, start pouring oil until mixture resembles a creamy sauce. Season with salt and pepper.

7. Fry shrimp tails in ½ cup olive oil. Add few drops of key lime, salt and pepper and continue frying until shrimp turn pink in color.

8. Serve ocopa sauce over slices of boiled potatoes, with hardboiled eggs, lettuce and olives.

9. Garnish with shrimp tails.

Anticuchos (Peruvian Chicken Kebabs)

Serves: 4

Ingredients:

Chicken kebabs:

- 2 chicken breast fillets cut into bite sized pieces
- kosher salt
- yellow pepper marinade

Yellow   pepper marinade:

- 2 cloves garlic minced
- 1 tablespoon aji amarillo paste (store bought or homemade)
- 1 tablespoon olive oil
- 1 teaspoon dried oregano
- ¼ tablespoon cumin
- ¼ black pepper

(Optional) homemade aji amarillo:

- 6-8 aji amarillo chiles (stemmed and deseeded) substitute 2 habanero and 1 large yellow bell pepper
- 3 tablespoons vinegar
- 1 tablespoon canola oil
- ¼ cup sugar

Method:

Aji amarillo paste:

1. Place chilis in a pot of cold water and bring to a boil. Reduce heat and simmer 30 minutes until ajis are soft.

Strain ajis and place in blender and add other ingredients. Blend to form a creamy paste. Strain in a mesh sieve.

Yellow pepper marinade:

1. Place all ingredients in bowl and mix well.

Chicken kebabs:

1. Marinate chicken in yellow pepper marinade for at least 30 minutes.
2. Remove pieces from marinade. Sprinkle with salt. Thread 3-4 pieces onto two skewers each.
3. Grill chicken kebabs on high heat about 4 minutes per side, brushing with the marinade.

Seco De Cerdo (Pork in Cilantro Sauce)

Serves: 10

Ingredients:

- 4 lb. 8 oz (2 k) pork meat (cut in medium size pieces)
- 8 medium-large yellow potatoes (peeled and cut in half)
- 2 onions (finely chopped)
- 2 garlic cloves (minced)
- 1 tablespoons ají amarillo fresco / fresh yellow aji (chili) blended
- 1 fresh or canned red pepper (seedless, cut julienne)
- 1 cup cilantro leaves (blended)
- 1 beef bouillon cube (dissolved in ½ cup hot water)
- 1 cup dry white wine
- 1 bottle of beer
- 1 carrot (diced)
- 1 cup fresh peas
- ¼ cup vegetable oil
- salt and pepper to taste

Method:

1. First, blend cilantro leaves with the necessary amount of water to obtain a thick puree.
2. Season pork with salt and pepper. Heat half of the oil in a heavy bottom pan, and brown pork meat evenly. Remove from pan.
3. Add rest of oil to the pan, if necessary, and sauté onion until almost done. Add garlic and cook for 1 minute. Add blended cilantro, peas and diced carrot. Cook stirring for

3 minutes. Add meat, bouillon, wine, beer, ají and red pepper. Season.

4. Combine well, stirring, cover pan and bring to a boil. Lower heat and simmer until meat is halfway cooked. Add potatoes and continue cooking. If potatoes are cooked before meat, remove from pan to prevent them from breaking.

5. Keep them warm until ready to use. Continue cooking, uncovered, until liquid evaporates and sauce thickens.

6. Return potatoes to pan, correct seasoning.

7. Serve with white rice, and fresh blended yellow aji on the side.

Chapter Four: Peruvian Dessert Recipes

Turron Doña Pepa (Anise Cookie Bar with Candy Syrup)

Serves: 6-8

Ingredients:

- 1 lb. cake flour
- 8 oz. (about 1 cup) vegetable shortening, very cold and cut in pieces
- 5 medium egg yolks
- 2 tablespoons sesame seeds (toasted and ground)
- 2 oz anise liquor
- 1 cup boiling water
- 1 tablespoon anise seeds
- ½ teaspoon salt
- candy sprinkles

Syrup:

- 6 cloves
- 2 cups water
- 2 pieces of molasses
- 2 quinces
- rind of 1 orange

Method:

1. First, preheat the oven to 350 F.
2. Put anise seeds in a cup and pour boiling water over them.
3. Put in the fridge until very cold.

4. In the working bowl of a food processor, pulse five or six times until everything looks like coarse oatmeal: flour, salt, and shortening. Transfer the mixture to a bowl and add the egg yolks, anise liquor and anise water, and sesame seeds.
5. Add anise water, tablespoon-by-tablespoon, mixing with a fork, until the dough holds together without being crumbly.
6. Put in the fridge until ready to use.
7. Divide in small portions (I used an ice cream scoop so all the pieces were the same size.)
8. Take a small portion.

Mazamorra Morada (Purple Corn Pudding)

Serves: 6-8

Ingredients:

- 2 lbs. (1 kg) purple corn
- 13 oz (400 g) sugar
- 12 dried peaches
- 12 prunes (pitted)
- 3 cinnamon sticks
- 3 cloves
- 2 apples (peeled and diced)
- 2 peaches (peeled and diced)
- 1 key lime (juiced)
- 1 quince (peeled and diced)
- 1 medium size pineapple (peeled, cored and diced)
- ¾ cup potato flour or cornstarch
- ½ currants
- ground cinnamon

Method:

1. First thing you need to do is soak the dried fruits overnight.
2. Place purple corn in a large pan with 12 cups of water together with the fruit peels, 2 cinnamon sticks, and 2 cloves. Boil for 20 minutes or until water turns into a deep purple color. Strain and keep purple corn water.
3. Drain dried fruits and combine with fresh fruits. Place them in a heavy bottom pan with 2 cups of the purple water, 2 cinnamon sticks and 1 clove. Bring to a boil. Add sugar and boil until fruit is tender. Strain liquid and combine with rest of purple corn water.

4. Remove cinnamon stick and clove from fruit, and return fruit to liquid. Add sugar to taste.
5. Dissolve potato flour or cornstarch in 2 cups of cold corn water.
6. Bring purple water and fruit to a boil and, gradually, add the cornstarch and the lime juice and stir until thickened. Cool.
7. Place pudding in a serving bowl or in individual cups. Sprinkle cinnamon on top.

Arroz Zambito (Dark Rice Pudding)

Serves: 4

Ingredients:

- 4 cloves
- 2 cups milk
- 2 cinnamon sticks
- 1 can evaporated milk
- 1 cup water
- 1 cup chancaca, coarsely chopped (or dark brown sugar)
- 1 teaspoon butter
- 1 teaspoon vanilla essence
- ½ teaspoon aniseed
- ½ cup arborio rice
- ½ cup grated dried coconut
- ½ cup raisins
- ½ cup pecans (toasted and chopped)
- ¼ teaspoon salt

Method:

1. First, put milk, cinnamon, cloves, aniseed, arborio rice, and salt in a heavy saucepan. Bring to a boil over medium heat, lower the heat, and simmer until the rice is al dente and the milk is almost evaporated, (about 20 minutes).
2. Add evaporated milk and water, chancaca, grated coconut, and raisins, and continue cooking over medium low heat until the chancaca melts, the rice is very soft, and the texture of the dessert is creamy, but still somewhat liquid.
3. Turn off the heat and discard the cinnamon sticks and the cloves.

4. Add butter and vanilla, stirring. Cool to room temperature.
5. Serve in nice glasses, and sprinkle with pecans.

Peruvian Alfajores with Manjar Blanco

Serves: 24

Ingredients:

- 2 ½ cups cornstarch
- 2 medium-large eggs
- 1 ½ sticks butter
- 1 cup white sugar
- 1 cup all-purpose flour
- 1 tablespoon and 1 ½ teaspoons pisco
- 1 teaspoon vanilla extract
- 1 tablespoon and 1 ½ teaspoons water (or as needed)
- 1 tablespoon confectioners' sugar (or as needed)
- ½ teaspoon baking powder

Manjar blanco:

- 2 tablespoons brown sugar
- 2 tablespoons confectioners' sugar (or to taste)
- 1 (14 ounce) can sweetened condensed milk
- ½ (6 ounce) can evaporated milk

Method:

1. First, preheat the oven to 300 F (150 C).
2. Beat white sugar and butter together in a large bowl using an electric mixer until creamy. Add cornstarch, flour, eggs, pisco, vanilla extract, and baking powder. Mix gently until combined.
3. Turn dough out onto a clean work surface and knead by hand until smooth. Add water as needed. Divide in half, refrigerate 1 portion, and leave the other out.

4. Coat your work surface with powdered sugar. Roll dough out to 1/4-inch thickness and cut into 2-inch rounds with a cookie cutter or shot glass. Place rounds close together on a baking sheet. Prick each cookie twice with a fork.
5. Bake in the preheated oven for 10 minutes; cookies should still be white and soft, not crispy, and will firm up as they cool. Repeat with remaining cookie dough.
6. Pour condensed milk, evaporated milk, and brown sugar into a saucepan over medium-low heat. Stir constantly until filling approaches the consistency of thick caramel, 20 to 30 minutes. Remove from heat; mixture will firm up as it cools to room temperature, about 30 minutes.
7. Pour confectioners' sugar into a shallow bowl. Spread about 1/2 tablespoon of the filling over cooled cookies. Attach every two cookies together to make the alfajores. Roll alfajores in confectioners' sugar.

Note:
- Use rum or vodka instead of pisco if desired.

Picarones (Sweet Potato Doughnut)

Serves: 6

Ingredients:

- 1,2 lb. sweet potatoes (peeled)
- 1,2 lb. squash (peeled)
- 1,2 lb. flour
- 4 cloves
- 3 tablespoons active dry yeast
- 3 tablespoons sugar
- 2 medium-large eggs (slightly beaten)
- 2 cinnamon sticks
- 2 tablespoons aniseed
- pinch of salt
- Oil (necessary amount for frying)

Syrup:

- 4 cloves
- 4 cups water
- 2 cinnamon sticks
- 2 allspice
- 2 cups molasses
- 1 cup brown sugar
- peel of 1 orange (cut into thick large strips)

Method:

1. First, fill water in a large pan with cinnamon, clove and aniseed. Boil for 10 minutes, approximately and strain reserving water.

2. Cook sweet potatoes and squash in the reserved water until tender. Remove from pan and force through a strainer. Reserve 2 cups of cooking liquid. Allow to cool.
3. In a small size bowl, combine yeast, sugar, and reserved cooking liquid. Set aside for 15 minutes.
4. Place strained sweet potatoes and squash in a large bowl. Add salt, yeast mixture and eggs. Stir vigorously until combined. Fold in flour and continue stirring until a soft and smooth and elastic dough is formed. Dough will not stick to fingers.
5. Cover with a damp cloth and leave dough to rise for 1 hour or until mixture doubles its volume.
6. Heat oil in a large skillet until hot. Take a small quantity of dough and form a ring. Fry in hot oil until golden on both sides. Repeat the procedure until all dough is used. Wet hands in salted water frequently to make dough rings more manageable.
7. Remove picarones from hot oil and drain in kitchen paper.
8. Serve immediately with syrup.

Syrup:

1. Combine molasses, sugar, clove, cinnamon, orange peel, allspice and water in a medium size saucepan.
2. Bring to a boil over low heat until mixture thickens to a syrup (200 °F / 110 °C). This process will take approximately 20 to 25 minutes.

Suspiro Limeno (Peruvian Custard)

Serves: 6

Ingredients:

- 1 (14 ounce) can sweetened condensed milk
- 1 (12 fluid ounce) can evaporated milk
- 2 egg yolks (beaten)
- 2 egg white (beaten)
- 1 tablespoon vanilla extract
- 1 cup confectioners' sugar
- ¼ teaspoon ground cinnamon (optional)

Method:

1. First, whisk together the sweetened condensed milk, evaporated milk, vanilla, and egg yolks in a saucepan. Place over medium-low heat and gently cook until the mixture thickens, stirring constantly with a wooden spoon, about 30 minutes. Pour into a heatproof serving dish and set aside.
2. Whip the egg whites with confectioners' sugar to stiff peaks *(see note)*. Spread meringue on top of milk mixture. Refrigerate until cold, about 3 hours.
3. Sprinkle with cinnamon before serving, if desired.

Note:
- To pasteurize your egg whites, you can make a Swiss meringue: combine the 2 egg whites with about ½ cup granulated sugar in a stainless-steel mixing bowl. Heat over a double boiler, stirring constantly, until sugar is melted and egg whites are hot to the touch. Remove from heat and whip until fluffy and stiff.

- Alternately, you can substitute ¼ cup pasteurized liquid egg whites and save the raw egg whites for another use. Pasteurized whites take longer to whip, but will work just fine.

Fruit Espuma (Gelatin Foam)

Serves: 5

Ingredients:

- 1 ½ cups water
- 1 (6 ounce) package raspberry flavored Jell-O mix
- 1 (12 fluid ounce) can very cold evaporated milk

Method:

1. First, bring water to a boil in a small saucepan. Stir in gelatin until completely dissolved, then place into refrigerator until cool (but not solid).
2. Pour evaporated milk into a large bowl, and whip with a hand mixer until fluffy and doubled in volume. While continuing to beat, slowly pour in cooled gelatin. When all of the gelatin has been incorporated, pour the mixture into a mold or bowl and chill until set, about 3 hours.
3. Once set, serve garnished with raspberries.

Tres Leches (Peruvian Three Milks)

Serves: 8

Ingredients:

Cake:

- 200g all-purpose flour
- 200g white sugar
- 100ml whole milk
- 4 medium eggs
- 1 teaspoon baking powder
- 1 teaspoon vanilla extract

Syrup   for soaking:

- 1 can (400g) sweetened condensed milk
- 300ml evaporated milk
- 300ml whole milk
- 1 dash of rum

Topping:

- 250ml whipping cream
- 50g sugar
- ½ teaspoon vanilla extract
- cinnamon

Method:

1. Start by preheating the oven to 175°C.
2. Lightly grease a square or rectangular cake or baking pan with a high edge. Sift flour and baking powder together and set aside. Separate the eggs.

3. Beat the egg whites in a mixing bowl until stiff. Then gradually add the sugar and whisk until the sugar is completely dissolved. Add the egg yolks and a teaspoon vanilla extract and beat until foamy. Gently fold in the flour-baking powder mixture, alternating with 100ml of milk until the batter is smooth.

4. Pour the batter into prepared baking dish and bake for around 30 minutes (or until a toothpick inserted in the center comes out clean). Allow to cool, and then pierce cake from all sides several times with a fork or skewer.

5. Whisk the sweetened condensed milk, the evaporated milk, the whole milk and the rum until well blended. Pour the liquid slowly and evenly over the cake until soaked (you don't need the entire amount). Cover with cling film and refrigerate for an hour. Soak the cake again with the syrup and keep covered for at least 3 hours (best overnight) in the fridge. Refrigerate the rest of the syrup as well.

6. Whip the cream, 50g of sugar and ½ teaspoon vanilla extract until stiff. Spread the cream over the top of cake and sprinkle with cinnamon. Serve cut into small squares together with the rest of the syrup.

Pie de Limon (Peruvian Lime Pie)

Serves: 4

Ingredients:

Crust:

- 200g all-purpose flour
- 80g soft butter
- 60g sugar
- 1 medium-large egg

Filling:

- 4 egg yolks
- 1 tin (400g) sweetened condensed milk

Meringue:

- 160g sugar
- 4 egg whites
- 1 pinch of salt

Method:

1. First, prepare the crust. Place the butter, flour, sugar and the egg into a bowl and blend together with an electric mixer. With your hands combine the mixture until you have a shiny dough. Then roll the pastry (best use some cling film or baking paper on top and bottom to avoid sticking). Place the pastry in a pie pan covering bottom and sides and refrigerate for 30 minutes. Pierce cold pastry several times with a fork and bake at 180°C for 10 minutes.

2. Meanwhile, prepare the filling. Whisk the egg yolks. Then add the sweetened condensed milk and the lime

juice and blend well. Pour the mixture on top of the pre-baked pastry and bake for another 10 minutes.

3. For the meringue beat the egg whites with a pinch of salt until very stiff. Gradually add the sugar and whisk until the sugar is completely dissolved and the meringue is creamy and shiny. Spread the meringue on top of the lime filling and bake another 10 minutes.

4. Serve cold.

Crema Volteada (Peruvian Crème Caramel)

Serves: 5

Ingredients:

Caramel sauce:

- 180 g sugar
- 3 tablespoons water
- squeeze of lime juice

Custard:

- 500 ml fresh whole milk
- 170 g sugar
- 4 medium eggs
- 4 medium egg yolks
- 1 teaspoon vanilla extract

Method:

Preparation of the Caramel Sauce:

1. Start by buttering the sides of the 5 ramekins and set aside. Pour the sugar and 3 tablespoons of water into a stainless-steel pan. Place the pot on medium heat and constantly stir with a wooden spoon. As soon the sugar is dissolved, stop stirring otherwise the sugar will crystalize. Add a squeeze of lime juice and let boil.

2. After a few minutes the sugar water turns into a nice caramel sauce. Once the caramel has a golden brownish color, remove from heat immediately. Make sure it's not getting too dark; else your caramel sauce tastes bitter. Quickly pour the sauce into the prepared ramekins. Set aside and let cool.

Preparation of the Custard:

1. Once your caramel sauce is prepared, pre-heat the oven to 175°C. In a large bowl, whisk the eggs and egg yolks until well combined and creamy. Gradually add the sugar and continue whisking until it's completely dissolved. Then pour in the milk and keep whisking. Stir in the vanilla essence.

2. Place the ramekins with the caramel sauce into a big enough oven-proof dish and fill them with the egg-milk mixture. Place the dish into the oven and pour boiling water into it until the ramekins are nearly completely covered.

3. Leave to bake for around 60 minutes. When the custard is properly set, take the crema volteada out of the oven and remove from the dish. Set aside to cool. Once cool place in the fridge until it's time for dessert (best overnight or at least a few hours).

4. To serve, just carefully loosen the edges with a knife and turn upside down on a plate.

Note:

- Often, crema volteada is made in a round baking pan with a hole in the middle. For a 24cm baking pan double above-mentioned ingredients.

Arroz con Leche (Peruvian Rice Pudding)

Serves: 2

Ingredients:

- 650 ml water
- 1 cup (200g) rice
- 1 tin (400 ml) evaporated milk
- 1 tin (400 ml) sweetened condensed milk
- 2 cloves
- 1 orange (juiced)
- 1 cinnamon stick
- 1 teaspoon vanilla essence
- cinnamon powder

Method:

1. First, pour the water into a heavy saucepan. Add the juice of one orange, the cinnamon stick and the cloves. Bring to a boil. Wash the rice thoroughly and add to the boiling water. Bring to a boil again. Then reduce heat and let simmer without lid until the water is gone and the rice is soft (about 15 – 20 minutes) Remove the cloves and the cinnamon stick.
2. Add the evaporated milk. Constantly stirring, bring to a boil, reduce heat and simmer continuing stirring until the mixture thickens (about 10 minutes).
3. Then add the sweetened condensed milk. Without stopping to stir, continue cooking over low heat until your rice pudding gets creamy (about 10 minutes). Stir in the vanilla essence.
4. Fill the rice pudding in a bowl or small glasses, sprinkle with cinnamon powder and serve hot or cold.

Suspiro a la Limena (Peruvian Caramel Pudding)

Serves: 4-6

Ingredients:

- 1 12-ounce can evaporated milk
- 1 14-ounce can sweetened condensed milk
- 3 medium-large eggs (yolks and whites separated)
- 2 tablespoons water
- 1 cup sugar or superfine sugar (if you prefer powdered sugar, use 1 ½ cups)
- ¼ cup Port wine
- ¼ teaspoon cinnamon

Method:

To make the custard:

1. Cook the evaporated milk and the sweetened condensed milk in a heavy saucepan over low heat, stirring constantly with a wooden spoon, until the mixture thickens to a smooth custard and turns a pale caramel color (about 30 minutes). Remove from the heat.
2. Whisk the egg yolks in a bowl. Add a couple of tablespoons of the hot custard and keep beating for a few seconds. Pour the egg mixture into the saucepan with the remaining custard and stir gently till blended. Let the custard cool to room temperature or chill in the fridge.

To make the meringue:

1. In a separate saucepan, mix the sugar, Port, and water over high heat. Bring to a boil for 6 minutes without

stirring. The syrup is ready when it forms a caramel thread that can be drizzled from a spoon.

2. Beat the egg whites with an electric beater at high speed until stiff peaks form.
3. Add the hot syrup in a thin and steady stream, beating until the resulting meringue is cool.

To make the meringue:

1. Fold the custard into individual cups and pipe meringue onto each serving. Or put all the custard in the bottom of a single serving dish and swirl the meringue across the entire surface. *(see note)*
2. Dust meringue lightly with cinnamon.
3. Serve at room temperature or chilled.

Note:

▪ To apply the meringue at its most decorative, use a pastry bag or make your own, by cutting an inch off the corner of a gallon plastic bag.

Peruvian Caramel Sandwich Cookies

Serves: 6

Ingredients:

- 1 cup all-purpose flour (plus extra for rolling)
- 1 vanilla bean (split in half lengthwise)
- 1 medium-large egg
- 1 jar dulce de leche
- ½ cup butter
- ½ cup granulated sugar
- ¼ teaspoon baking powder
- 1/8 teaspoon salt
- powdered sugar (optional)
- shredded unsweetened coconut (optional)

Method:

1. Sift the flour and baking powder into a medium bowl.
2. Add the salt, mix thoroughly and set aside.
3. Put the butter and sugar in the bowl of standing mixer with a whisk attachment.
4. Scrape the vanilla seeds from the vanilla bean into the bowl. (You can keep the pod in a container of sugar for vanilla sugar, if you like, instead of throwing it out.)
5. Cream together until the mixture is pale and fluffy.
6. Add the egg and mix until combined, scraping down the sides of the bowl.
7. Add the flour mixture in 2 batches until just combined.
8. Wrap the dough with plastic wrap and refrigerate for about 2 hours. You could also keep the dough in the freezer if you won't need the cookies for a few days, and it thaws pretty well, for a quick sweet treat.

9. Preheat the oven to 350°F.
10. Line 2 baking sheets with silicone baking mats.
11. Remove the dough from the fridge and unwrap. Using the extra flour and a rolling pin, roll the dough to about 1/8-inch thickness.
12. Using a round cookie cutter about 1 1/2 inches in diameter, cut circles from the dough and put them on the baking sheets.
13. Bake the cookies until pale gold; they will have a dry appearance on top when they are finished. Remove from the oven and allow to cool.
14. Place a teaspoon of Dulce de Leche in the center of every other cookie and sandwich together with the bare cookies. You could stop at this point, or roll the cookies sideways in the coconut and dust with powdered sugar.

Humitas de Mote (Dried Corn Humitas)

Serves: 8

Ingredients:

- 250g mote (dried corn)
- ½ - 1 cup oil
- ½ - 1 cup sugar
- ½ cup raisins
- corn husks

Method:

1. Soak the corn overnight.
2. When ready to make the humitas, grind the corn in a food processor until a paste forms and it's as thin as you can get it.
3. Mix sugar and oil into this paste, until you get a thick paste texture, and it's sweet enough for you.
4. Add raisins into the mixture.
5. Cover the base of a pan with shredded corn husks.
6. Put 2 tablespoons of dough in the center of each husks, and wrap forming a rectangle.
7. Put the humitas laying down in the pan, forming several layers.
8. Cover everything with more shredded corn husks, and add some water to the pan (2 - 3 cups would be enough).
9. Bring to a boil and cook, covered, at medium heat, for 25 minutes. Let cool for at least 10 minutes before serving.

Conclusion

I want to thank you once again for purchasing this book.

One of the world's most vibrant cultural experiences, Peruvian cuisine is the living legacy of a colourful history played out across south America.

Peruvian Food is an important expression of its own culture and history, considered in the same light as both its local music and literature. Full to the brim with amazing local ingredients and an incredible combination of local spices, Peruvian cooking is a site to behold.

And now you hold it in that palm of your hand!

With the help of recipes in this book, you will be able to create gourmet and authentic Peruvian food in no time at all – seriously, all you need to do is gather the ingredients and start cooking.

I strongly recommend you start this process by selecting a recipe that takes your fancy and begin experiment a little in the kitchen, and the next time you have guests over for a meal, you can blow them away!

So, thank you, and enjoy the journey!

Other Books by Grizzly Publishing

"Jamaican Cookbook: Traditional Jamaican Recipes Made Easy"

https://www.amazon.com/dp/B07B68KL8D

"Brazilian Instant Pot Cookbook: Delicious Pressure Cooked Meals Made Fast and Easy"

https://www.amazon.com/dp/B078XBYP89

"Norwegian Cookbook: Traditional Scandinavian Recipes Made Easy"

https://www.amazon.com/dp/B079M2W223

"Casserole Cookbook: Delicious Casserole Recipes From Around The World"

https://www.amazon.com/dp/B07B6GV61Q

Made in the USA
Coppell, TX
27 November 2022

87174204R00090